A COMPILATION OF HURRICANE KATRINA STORIES

A COMPILATION OF HURRICANE KATRINA STORIES

(Before, During and Aftermath)

Lucy Baker Wheelden

To order additional copies of this book, contact:
Xlibris Corporation
1-888-795-4274
www.Xlibris.com
Orders@Xlibris.com
41817

CONTENTS

Jo and Donny

Jo's Sixth Sense Burbank, CA

Some mornings are just like that. I woke up feeling like someone had taken my world and turned it upside down. Okay. I can deal with this for a day, but this went on for two weeks. It was the end of summer in Burbank, California. The wildfires were burning in the valleys around us and the air was hot and still, as well as smoke-filled. Maybe that's why I felt so depressed and lonely.

Donny, my husband, was working long hours trying to get the new audio studio complete. He couldn't record or teach without the studio. His job at church was the only income we had at this time, so I was concerned about our usual end of summer trip.

We took our son, Brendan, someplace special the weekend before school started. This year we'd gotten reservations for Knots Berry Farm, hotel and admission to the theme park. Bre was pretty hyped up for it. As he was going into Junior High, he said he was 'too old' for Disneyland anymore.

Why did I have this sinking feeling all day? I began to collect and itemize my things, as if I was worried about not having enough money for the trip. I could make money by selling on e-bay. The clothes I'd worn for different jobs on movie sets were only sentimental to me. They could go. The shoes. I had some I'd worn once and never put on again. (I'm a jeans and Reebok type). They went like hotcakes. I sold almost all my stuff, and looked around for more. Still the feeling something was wrong kept me awake at night.

Maybe Donny was leaving me. I felt so alone. I couldn't even think about what I'd do without him. We've been married for fifteen years, after all. I didn't want to think about it but at night, when I lay next to him staring at the ceiling, I'd think about it anyway. I mean I couldn't turn it off.

Whatever it was, it kept getting worse. I wasn't sure about anything anymore. Bre and I would go bike riding and I'd just keep pumping and not notice where we were going. He'd have to say, "This way, mom".

Thursday morning the National Weather Service reported that there was a powerful hurricane in the Gulf of Mexico. Her name was Katrina. She was headed to New Orleans, which was close to Granma's house in Donny's home town of Bay St. Louis, Mississippi.

I was in hopes that this was not my premonition coming to life. I started recording the beginning events, of the evacuation and people boarding-up their windows and stuff. All the while I was hoping this would be something I could add to our annual Christmas Bloopers DVD, with Granma laughing about a tree limb landing in her front yard.

On the Friday afternoon we arrived at Knots Berry Farm and checked into the hotel, Donny was on the telephone most of the time with different people about the studio. He was super busy, even on our mini-vacation. Bre ran into a friend from his class in the lobby, and they exchanged room numbers planned to hang out together at the park all day Saturday. I felt like excess luggage.

Here I was, alone again. I sat in the pavilion watching the boys as they went on rides and Donny sat at the table next to me. We had lemon aide and talked about the fires with the parents of the other kid. I enjoyed being out in pleasant company, but that nagging feeling simply wouldn't leave me. It just kept hanging on.

We returned on Sunday, in time for Donny go to work. He worked for the church all day. He was tired from our weekend out, but had an obligation to do the job. He filmed one service for the church files and also a live television service, which was broadcast to people's homes. There was always a live band and professional singers during each service. He had to adjust the sound and place microphones and stuff like that.

Bre and I hung out at home. He went to play with the kids out at the basketball goal and I sat inside feeling alone and depressed. What in the world was I going to do? I couldn't keep on like this, I knew.

When Donny arrived home that afternoon, I told him to call all of his relatives living on the Coast, and find out their plans for evacuating. When we heard everyone was going to stay and ride it out, we were very concerned, to say the least. But Granma's calm attitude, and the fact that she and Rob had gone through Hurricane Camille, made me hopeful everything would be okay.

That night was good. We'd planned a neighborhood Bar-b-Q for Monday with the other families in our apartment complex, as we do every year. It's our "Labor Day Do". Donny checked that we had all the stuff we needed for his cook-out. He and Bre went over to Pravilion to get pickles and more eggs. His Cajun potato salad was the greatest, but he insisted on fresh eggs every time.

I made some cookies and cupcakes with Bre telling me how to spell the kids names I put on the cookies with icing. I may not be the best cook in the world, but I can bake up some pretty tasty cookies!

I felt all empty inside, in spite of all I ate at the cook out. It was as though I was just going through the motions, waiting for something awful to happen. Not knowing what was the bad part. I thought of all the things it could possible be from Brendan getting sick to Donny running away with a young floozy (Hey, you never know). It was just that I just felt all alone, even though I was where I belonged, in the heart of my family.

Later that night, I couldn't stand it anymore. As Donny and I sat on the couch watching the late news, I said. "I think something bad is going to happen. Maybe not to us directly, but maybe with Granma."

I just needed some release and it felt good to share it with someone else. Not really being a practicing Christian, I prayed that night for a sign. I was desperate for this nagging feeling to cease once and for all.

"God, just give me a sign." I prayed with all my heart as I went to bed Sunday night. And I swear. within ten minutes I watched lightening flash over my bedroom and heard a loud, rolling thunder that even woke Donny from his usual heavy sleep.

"Oh, a storm," I thought. "That's it! The rain will help put out the fires."

I lay back in bed and slept like a baby. I was relaxed and felt like my old self again when I woke up Monday morning. I took a shower, brushed my teeth and dressed, happy to be back to my normal self again.

However, it wasn't over. It was just beginning.

I spent the day on the couch watching CNN, FOX and MSNBC. I watched in a daze as the circle of the storm kept getting bigger and deeper purple by the hour. I couldn't believe I was looking at an American City when they showed New Orleans. The levee had broken and the water was everywhere. They even showed dead bodies floating around. I watched people inside the Super Dome. I heard reports of the Charity Hospital there and saw pictures of people and animals stranded on the rooftops.

Feelings of guilt swept over me about not ever visiting that part of the States. I'd never known what it was like before Katrina, only what she left behind.

As news of New Orleans came in all day I waited for a report on Grandma's area. As a journalist, I felt they were either avoiding it because it was really bad, or they just couldn't get anyone out there to report on it.

My cell phone was glued in one hand and the remote in the other. I kept calling Grandma's number, thinking she would pick up and say, "Hay, Jo. I'm here and we're all doing fine!" But that didn't happen.

Tuesday, August 30th was even worse. They showed the people of New Orleans stranded in their homes, on the highway and inside the Super Dome,

That's when I decided to go on the local Mississippi bulletin boards and start listing everyone's names as missing. I really didn't know if they had survived the wrath of Hurricane Katrina. Never in a million years did I ever think I'd be doing such a thing. It was a very surreal moment in my life. I was literally one person of thirty when the list began and I sat in front of my computer screen and watched in horror as that list increased to thirty thousand people by weeks' end!

Most news stations were showing people asking about their loved ones, giving out their phone numbers and locations, hoping someone would hear their plea. I went online to the NASA facility in Hancock County (where our folks live). I requested if the list of those seeking shelter there bore the names of our kin. Bingo! I got a hit on Teddy, Niny and Baby Ziena Baker. Now I only had to worry about Granma, Pawpaw Tom, Rob and his family.

It wasn't until four days after the storm that we were able to see the destruction left by Katrina. I had found footage on a local internet site in Gulfport (WLOX.com) A news helicopter had captured the devastation up and down the Coast. I was in awe of Mother Nature and the power she holds over us. I called Brendan into the room to take a look and I also called Donny at the studio. I warned him about what he was going to see, but he wanted to see it firsthand.

As we sat there watching the camera sweep across the towns along the Gulf Coast, it was like looking at a battlefield. Everything that hadn't been swept away by the storm was broken and strewn about. We'd had our American Tsunami!

As we sat there watching, I remember saying, "It'll be a miracle if Grandma survived this horrific event, but it could happen. After all, they had been pulling 100-year-old Grandmas out of buildings in New Orleans.

It wasn't but two minutes after that statement that my cell phone chirped with a text message from Grandma's cell phone. I read, "we r all ok".

Thank goodness our Grandma knows how to text message! She says she inherited Donny's technical skills. She also says you can't kill Crab Grass.

Two days later, Grandma was finally able to call us and confirm she and Grandpa Tom were okay, as well as Donny's two brothers and their families. Although everyone's home was totally destroyed, or just plain gone, the important thing was they were all safe.

Brendan, Katrina Relief

G'ma and PawPaw

My Story of Hurricane Katrina

I felt safe that night, going to bed on Sunday, August 28th, 2005. Our house is on a high spot along the Gulf Coast. There had never been water there during any pro-ceding storms, and they'd been a few really bad ones in the last seventy years, I can tell you first-hand. Even though we live only a block and a half from the Gulf of Mexico.

The local news station (Mike Reader of WLOX) kept repeating that it was a big storm, and if you live in the areas indicated in red in the phone book, mandatory evacuation was not necessary, but advisable.

We'd filled the tanks of both cars, but after seeing the traffic jams on I-10, and the horror stories of people running out of gas and being shoved to the shoulder of the road to allow others to pass, or becoming ill and not being able to get to help, we decided to stay.

Hurricane Katrina was south of Port Sulfur, Louisiana West of the Mississippi River. The storm would have to cross the boot of Louisiana to get to Mississippi Gulf Coast. It was predicted to follow the river northward toward Baton Rouge.

My son and his wife had taken their two-year-old daughter to the shelter at NASA. No pets were allowed, so they left Quincy, their Yorkshire terrier with us. We all went to sleep, confident that we were safe.

My cell phone woke me up Monday morning when the electricity went out. I got out the portable radio (which we'd equipped with fresh batteries) and tried to get a local station. All I could get was Pensacola or New Orleans. My husband went on the back porch to make coffee on the gas burner of the cooker there. No news sounded good. I was trying to make out the problem when he came back in with a cup in each hand.

We sat at the counter in the kitchen as the wind became increasingly stronger. Branches and other stuff began hitting the tin roof overhead. The rain came down in sheets. I sipped my coffee and made sure Quincy had fresh water and dog food.

My daughter in law, Niny, called from the shelter to see how we were doing and assure us they were just fine. As we spoke, the phone went dead and I knew the towers were blowing down. The radio was no good to us locally, as they started ranting on about the levee breaking in New Orleans.

Yes, that was earth-shattering news, but didn't help us here in Bay St. Louis. Tom went to refill our cups and check the boards over the windows and glass doors in the front of the house. I was having a hissy fit, with him out there in the wind with tree branches, pieces of houses and only God knew what else flying around in 160 mph winds.

There was a gurgling noise from the bathroom, and I got up to see what was happening. The sewerage was backing up into the tub and toilet. As I stood in the hallway watching all that fecal matter and gagging on the odor, I heard a tremendous crunching crash from my bedroom. As I looked toward the bay window, I saw the baseboard crack open and water gushed in, making a hole in the wall under the window as it did.

Standing first ankle deep, then knee deep in the nasty water, I grabbed a towel and one of the baby's old quilts when I saw Quincy swimming toward me with fear in his black eyes. I scooped him up and wiped him down with the towel before swaddling him in the quilt. He buried his nose in it, because it smelled like his little mistress. I held him on my shoulder and waded to the front room where I sat on the sofa. Wind howled down the chimney like a seven-hundred-pound wolf. Things bumped against the sides of the house and crashed down upon the rooftop. Tom joined me there and we watched the water climb higher on the leaded glass of the front door.

"We better move, Hon," Tom said. "It's going to get deeper and my butt's getting wet."

He guided me into the kitchen. We couldn't see what was going on outside. Sitting on the bar stools at the breakfast counter holding a quivering dog in my arms, I felt numb. The radio was silent, but everything else was roaring, howling and generally making a lot of noise.

Tom and I looked at each other. He reached out a hand and I put mine in it. We could feel the love of God all around us right in our own kitchen as the water lapped higher. It was like a warm shawl around both of us and we felt loved and protected.

"Whichever way it turns out," Tom said. "We'll be together."

"Either way, Hon, I'm with you," I answered. "Whatever God has planned for us, we can trust him."

The water stopped right below the seat of the stools. The cat jumped from the table to the buffet to the back of the TV set on its stand. When she jumped for the counter she missed by this much. I found out that cats could swim. She went around the counter and Tom opened the door for her. She swam out onto the porch.

We sat there for I don't know how long. We touched each other occasionally. His fingertips on the back of my hand, my hand on his strong knee as I shifted in my chair. We said, "I love you" quite a few times, but neither would put words to what was really running thorough our minds.

"We're okay, but what about the kids?"

There was no communication going on anywhere around us now. We were totally alone in the middle of a fierce storm with floodwaters and tornadoes thrown in for good measure. The boards over the bay window of the dining room, the dark clouds and rumbling thunder and the constant howling of the wind in the chimney were enough to scare a sane person to death. I couldn't imagine what poor Niny was going through. She wasn't from the coast, and had no idea how intense it could rage. I hoped she and Ted were okay in the shelter.

Robert wouldn't have gone to the shelter, because he and Sherida have seven dogs, three cats, two birds, a pet squirrel and a boa, not to mention the two salt-water tanks of fish. They also lived two miles inland. Surely they weren't having flooding that far on shore, I hoped not, anyway.

Sherida had sent the children to the shelter at NASA with her mom and dad. They might even be playing with Baby Ziena now, I thought. Niny hadn't mentioned seeing them when she'd called this morning, but we'd been cut off, so maybe?

The water started going down. Tom said he had to open the back door to let it out. I sat holding Quincy awhile, and then noticed the water level through the glass panes of the garden doors leading from my kitchen to the living room. It was a good foot higher in the living room then the kitchen. I placed Quincy in the folds of the baby blanket on my stool and waded over to open the doors so the glass panes wouldn't break.

When I pushed them open the water rushed out in a wave. Something hit my shins and knocked me off my feet. The strong undertow drug me across the kitchen to the back door, where Tom grabbed me in his arms as items went whipping past us in the receding wave.

He put me back on my feet with both arms around me. We held the embrace for the warmth and strength we felt from each other. I put my arms around his neck and we kissed as the Gulf of Mexico ran out of our house and the storm raged on.

Quincy whined and we broke apart to take care of him. I don't know what happened to the cat. Exhausted, we went into the front room and flopped on sofa and recliner. It was wet, and you could hear the water draining out of the padding and upholstery, as we lay limp and spent.

My beautiful new hardwood floor was muddy with the bottom of the Gulf of Mexico deposited in scattered sand bars around the living room. Little puddles of water stood in some places between drifts of sandy silt.

"Looks like we could go floundering in here," I commented.

"Leave it, hon." Tom's voice reflected his weariness. "The insurance company will send someone out to clean up just like they did after the fire."

The all day storm left us exhausted and emotionally drained. We said our prayers and fell asleep where we lay. Two old folks together in the house that his daddy had built. It held together pretty good, in spite of the best Mother Nasty could throw at it. Good for you, Pappy.

How helpless we are without things which didn't exist in Hurricane Camile, 38 years earlier. So we couldn't use our cell phones because the towers were down. The internet was not a choice for us, either, because the electricity was off all over the Coast, and I'm sure the cable was, too. Here it was, the hottest month of the summer, and we had no air conditioning or fans.

The absolute worse was not being able to get in touch with our children. Those who live here to see how they faired, and those away to let them know we made it through the storm. The news we are able to get on the portable radio sounds as though the entire Gulf Coast (all the way north to Hattiesburg) is divastated. Much worse than Camille. They're saying it's the most distructive storm in America's history.

The next morning, I wanted to let the kids know I was alright, so I put our American Flag out. They'd know, if they saw airial shots from the many helicopters and private planes flying over, that we were still here. My dad used to put out his flag to let us know when he and mom were at the summer place, and I was in hopes the kids would remember, anyway. Much later, when I got in touch with my daughter-in-law in Burbank, CA, I asked if she had seen it.

"The first shots we saw of Bay St. Louis was from one such reporter in a helicopter," she informed me. "He said, 'What a patriotic town. Everyone has American Flags flying from their houses.' But we'd heard from you by then, so we knew you and Dad were alive."

I was standing in the kitchen, wondering how I was ever going to clean up the mess, when the back door burst open. My son, Rob came rushing in, grabbed me and hugged me so hard my ribs protested. I was so glad to see him I cried. I didn't know at that time what he and Sherida had gone through. It was a blessing just to hold my boy in my arms again.

He told me he was going to Texas with his wife and kids until things were more livable here in Bay St. Louis. The kids' school was damaged beyond repair at this time, and they needed to get into school. He needed to get away and think of what he wanted to do, as well.

Ted and Niny came home around noon. Baby Ziena was very upset over the devastation. Ted, Niny, Pawpaw and I had a group hug and cried. Each of us thought the other might have been lost forever. Praise God, we are all safe. There must have been zillions of prayers from all over the world going up to God during that storm. We were left with so few fatalities in this storm. It could have been so much worse if it had been at night.

Ted, Niny and I worked hard to get the mess out of the house. Although there was no running water, Ted's skiff had floated up to the side gate and we dipped our buckets in it to clean the mud off the floors. I was trying to save my hardwood floor I'd just had installed. The sofas were ruined with the mud and water (not to mention all the sewerage which had backed up and flowed out with the seawater). Ted helped me put them out front. Other things I put out to be cleaned. After a long exhausting day, Ted set up an air mattress in the kitchen.

We slept like babies.

Bridget Maurigi, Bayou La Croix, Mississippi

I live alone on the bayou with my horses. Some friends invited me to stay at their house up in Kiln for the storm. It was better than being all by myself. I am an unmarried lady over 21, and live my own choice of life. I work hard in construction, and party hearty with the guys after work.

Monday, August 29th, 2005 the storm hit at five in the morning. The winds and tornadoes were so loud. The trees were popping and whipping around. Some were uprooted by the winds and hit the ground with a house shaking 'thump'. All the power lines and poles were getting blown down. The roof lifted up and lots of rain poured inside the house, driven by hurricane force winds. We huddled together in fear and misery, wet and scared, not knowing if it would ever end, or if we'd be around to see the results when it did.

We got at least 6" rain inside the house. The hurricane lasted till five-thirty that evening.

All the guys got chain saws, got their ATVs, 4-wheelers and big trucks, and began moving everything they could. They tried to free up the roads so we could drive out, but trees, trailers, houses and pieces of fencing, plastic and tin roofing cluttered the way. They just kept on sawing and towing stuff off the road.

We couldn't get our cell phones to work. There was nothing coming in on the portable radio, either. On Tues. Aug. 30th, I was told everyone in Bay St. Louis & Waveland was dead. My mother and brother lived there. I was about to have a heart attack, but I didn't. It hurt so bad not knowing if they were dead or alive, my chest felt like it had a heavy chain around, squeezing it.

When we could finally get through, I drove down Highway 603 toward my house to see if there was anything left of it. The place was sealed off and I was not allowed on my property. The Corpse of Engineers and some National

Guardsmen were there. They told me there had been thirty-eight feet of water in that section and they were looking for bodies. They found seven in my attic and two on the premises. A total of nine bodies were found, at that time. I never found out who they were or how they happened to choose my house to seek shelter. Later, in October, I was once again prevented from going on my land because they found one more body there. That was a total of ten bodies found on my property. They didn't even count my horses. They were just animals, I guess.

I went on to Bay St. Louis to see if my Mom was okay. She had been alone, except for her dog Bear. The water came up to four feet in her house, and Bear got her out of the house and on top of my '94 Firebird, which was parked in her driveway. That's where she rode out the storm. I hugged her neck and we both cried. My brother, Robert, was doing good, too, but his back was hurt.

People in the country didn't have a way to get t0 town, and the hot August weather was very hard on them. I gave rides to people who were walking with babies and they all were just so pitiful looking. One young mother with a baby on her hip, a little one holding her hand and pregnant with another one was walking down the highway barefoot and all alone. I offered her a ride, she said, "I ain't got noplace to go." I took her and the kids to the Red Cross tent in front of K-Mart. I started hauling ice and water to the people in the country who I knew didn't have a car to come get it. I did whatever I could to try and help who ever needed it.

We started working on Eddie's house late Sept. Brother Benny, who is a Baptist preacher from Virginia, showed up. He stayed there also. Every morning I went down to Eddie's and Brother Benny would be saying prayer and I would just stop and listen. Finally, in October after putting Eddies roof on, Mr. Woody brought Dr. Hanawalt to Eddie's, introduced him to Brother Benny and all the rest of us. Dr. Hanawalt was the pastor of the First Presbyterian Church in Bay St. Louis. He was organizing workers to direct the flow of volunteers that poured in from all over America to help the victims of the storm. He talked with our crew and Brother Benny said he would come down and help as soon as we got finished with this job here.

He left & Brother Benny asked me to go into the FEMA trailer. As he led me to the Lord, I found the strength to quit drinking and was so happy to become a child of God. It's been great for me since the storm, as I have met lots of brothers and sisters. It's good to be a part of a Church family. I don't feel alone anymore. I'm working to help put our community back together, and I know Jesus is pleased with my life now.

Everyone, I just want to thank God and all of you for everything you've done and for your support. Pastor Jones says an elephant came and sat on Hancock County, Mississippi, and each of you has taken a bite out of that elephant. Soon it will be all gone, and we'll be back to normal. I'll never be back to the person I used to be, thanks to Brother Benny and other Christians leading me the right way.

Rob and Sherida

Rob's Story

I guess most people forty are middle-aged. My teen kids tease me I'm over-the-hill. I work hard at my job of house construction. I don't drink or smoke cigarettes, because I know I don't want to end up with DTs and Lung Cancer. Okay, so I pump up, too. What's wrong with a guy lookin' good?

My wife is short and Grandma Lydia always called her "that skinny girl" when she couldn't remember her name, which seemed like all the time to me. She is my lady. We dated, then lived together and finally got married. She made an honest man outta me, in spite of myself. She has three kids from her first marriage and they came to live with us once we ot settled in Bay St. Louis. We got a good thing going with our friendship as well as real love. It's been a lotta years, so I know the initial chemistry must'a wore off by now, although sometimes I don't think so.

Sherida works at a vet's office three days a week. She brought home a dog that had been boarded there for a few weeks. She said the storm might be bad in Pass Christian, so didn't want to leave Joey there alone. We already had six dogs, a Boston terrier, one mutt and four Boxers (a money-maker gone south). What's one more?

Her mom came and picked up the kids to take them to the shelter at NASA. We couldn't go because you can't take dogs to a shelter. We not only had seven dogs, we also have 3 cats, two birds, a pet squirrel, a boa constrictor and two salt-water aquariums. My lady takes her animals seriously.

Stephany, cried when we told her she was going to a shelter with Mawmaw. She is twelve, and the youngest of the three. I call her Baby Girl. She's going through her melodramatic stage, I think. You know, the kind where you tell her she can't go to the skating rink and she runs to her room screaming, slams the door and cries very loud for about three hours. Oh, well. Maybe she'll outgrow it soon.

The guys were being frisky and goofing off with each other instead of getting their stuff like I told them, so I had to "hup' them up a bit while

Sherida dealt with the sobbing and slobbering kisses from Baby Girl. I made sure each had a change of underclothes, toothbrushes, underarm deodorant and snacks. Kris and Micah ran out to Maw Sharon's pickup and got in the back seat. Baby Girl came out sniffling and carrying a well-packed plastic bag. She gave her Mom one last hug and got in the front seat by Mawmaw Sharon.

"Good bye. Love you," we all yelled at one another as the truck went down the road toward Highway 603 to Stennis Space Center where they'd ride out Hurricane Katrina. Mama and me got busy getting stuff battened down and put away so the wind wouldn't catch it.

"Did you get the water?" "Yeah, it's on top the kitchen counter. Did you fill the bathtub?" "Not yet. I want a good bath, first." "You got more candles?" "No, I forgot. You got enough Coleman Lanterns around here, must be *one* that works." "Not anymore. I made my mom a bird feeder out of it."

And it went on like that while we worked at preparations and kept up with Mike Reader on WLOX TV. I put some pork chops in my smoker and Sherida put potatoes and eggs on to boil for the potato salad. I got a Creole tomato from our garden, washed it and slapped it with Blue Plate, salt and pepper. It's all good.

We got tired of watching the same-ole, same-ole on TV, so I popped in a movie and Sherida made the popcorn and opened me a Dr. Pepper. We kicked back totally sated and relaxed. We were ready for that ole hurricane.

I woke up to the dogs braying. I mean, think about seven dogs all giving the warning signal at one time. It was a fast wake up, I can tell you. It was coming light and the wind was blowing like a son-or-a-gun. I went out and stood leaning into it, trying to outguess the storm. The pine trees in the churchyard across the road were whipping back and forth in the wind. The clouds were building up out of the Southeast. Bad stuff, right out of the Gulf of Mexico.

I *really* knew we was in trouble when I saw the sheet of water come across the churchyard toward my house. It was grayish-brown and it wasn't long until I was seeing whitecaps in my front yard. I ran for the house, yelling for Sherida to get the birdcages up in the attic. I was pulling the stairs down and packing our animals up into the attic in a frantic hurry. All I could think about was getting them up high.

The cats didn't wait for an invitation, Butter, Lucky and CeeCee came up with little urging, and climbed into the overhead rafters. The birdcages were on either side toward the back so as to leave room for me and Sherida and the seven dogs.

I was on the last pup when I looked down at my wife. She was sweaty and full of dog hair, but she was the most beautiful thing in my life. I got tears in my eyes just thinking about how much I love her. Then I noticed the water was up to her breast. She tossed her head back and gave me a big ole smile.

"Well, get your butt on up there, cowboy. I need to get up, too, you know." she said.

I could see out the front window from where I squatted on the ladder to the attic. The water outside was a good two feet higher than what we had inside. I looked into the attic. The animals were snug, they had water and different foods. Then I noticed the spiders climbing up all over the place from the inside walls of the house.

"We're in trouble," I told Sherida as I made my way through the mucky water to the front door. "We gotta get outta here *now!*"

I told Sherida to hang onto the bookcase, cause the water level was about to change. I took in a deep breath, braced my foot against the door jam and pulled with all my might. It took three tries, but the door finally gave just before I was going to give up. We went under the carport and hung onto the rafters. The tin roof above us was making a big racket. Sherida was crying, "What's going to happen to us?" and her purse came floating out of the house right up to her. She grabbed it and held it on her arm as the roof flew off the carport, one tin sheet at a time and sounded like a big saw blade twanging.

"We gotta go up, Babe," I said, and pulled her toward me. She was slick as a peeled onion. "What you got on, Hon. You're mighty slick."

"You and your saved grease!" She fussed at me. "It all came drifting out the kitchen and got me when I was taking the dogs out their crates and up to the ladder. I feel like a greased pig."

"We gotta go up anyhow. Just be careful not to get cut on the tin roof." I said, and helped her over to the corner of the carport by the house. She climbed up on the edge of the roof and held on. Stuff was flying all around her and she kept her eyes squeezed shut. I hoisted myself up behind her and we hunkered down on the side of the roof away from the wind.

The water just kept getting higher. I realized that the house was swaying under us. I didn't think it was going to stand up to this baby. I looked around to see what I could do. There was a keg. A old wooden keg, just the right size to put over Sherida to keep her from getting tore up by all this flying stuff. I would swim out and get it for her.

I had to swim past my shed, and prayed to God I didn't run into anything like the tin roofing I had stored. I'm a keeper. I knew what was in there, and it made me swim *very* carefully, and not do a deep kick, for fear of getting sliced and diced. I got the keg. It was empty, and I didn't have any trouble getting back to my Lady. I held the keg over her and looked around.

The Sunday school building across the street was almost all the way underwater. I looked the other way. My boat bobbed along almost submerged. I had filled it with water so the wind wouldn't catch it and toss it around. She was not going to last long, but then, neither were we if I didn't do something.

"Sherida. I'm going for the boat." I said. "Keep the keg on so you don't get hurt, hear me?"

"Love you." She mouthed, as she took the keg off and held it against her chest. I went in, knowing I had to pass the Magnolia tree and hoping I didn't get hung up in its branches. I was swimming against the wind, and it was hard. I got the boat, made sure the plug was in, then swam it back to the roof where Sherida sat holding the keg.

The roof swayed. "Get in!" I yelled over the howling wind.

Sherida got into the middle of the boat where she usually sat when we went out on the River fishing. The water washed over the gunnel. She was up to her waist in water in the boat.

I saw a big plastic McDonald's cup. I lunged out and got it. Sherida was bailing the water out the boat with both hands. I dipped in the cup and between us we got it up enough so's I could roll in. I lay there, so tired and my neck hurt. I don't even know what time it was. I only knew this storm went on too dang long.

Sherida screamed we were being carried away on the water. I took the steering cable out the front and grabbed onto a pine tree as we passed it. I tied up good, then held the keg over Sherida again. Now we were being whipped up by the pine branches, as well as everything else the storm could pick up and fling at us. I don't know where all the stuff came from, but it was really scary when a rooftop flew toward us and made a tidal wave where it hit down beyond us in the surf. Propane tanks, life jackets plastic and Styrofoam ice chest. I felt like the water was boiling under us while the freezing rain pelted us from the side. The wind howled and screamed. Sherida and I just held on and hoped.

It went on and on and on. It was daytime, but the sky was so black with clouds and rain it looked like dusk. I couldn't tell what time it was or anything. The stuff you see floating past you in a flood is unreal. I saw a old-fashioned baby buggy, with lacy pillow float pass. I saw tires blowing on top of the waves like a surfboard. The trucks floated and I was real worried about the animals. The water was so high, only the ridgeline of the Sunday school building was visible above the water. Would they be okay? I hoped so, but had to worry about my lady most of all.

I don't know when the water turned. I know when the angle of the boat almost tipped us out it was time to make our move. Sherida threw away the keg and started swimming toward the house as the top of the open front door came into view. Her purse on her arm, and her long legs hardly making a ripple as she swam to it. I was right behind her.

"Roary! Gin! Boy!" Sherida was yelling as soon as she got inside the house. "Oh, Butter. I hope ya'll made it."

I was too tired to yell anything. I saw Ginger looking out the open attic hole at the top of the stairs. We went up to a damp attic. Sherida checked all the animals and said she thought they all made it except for the birds, the squirrel and the boa. "The Salt-water fish should do alright in this water, as it is brackish." she said, as she lay on the floor beside Roary and put her head against his big blocky one. I found a plastic bag of clothes and undid the twist tie. I threw her a sweatshirt and took one for myself. It was cold after being in the water all day and the wind was still flapping the tin roof overhead, making it real drafty. I pulled off my wet shirt and put on one, too. I put my head on the plastic bag of clothes and just before I dropped off, I saw Ditto puke up water, so I guess she came pretty near drowning.

I couldn't help her. I went to sleep.

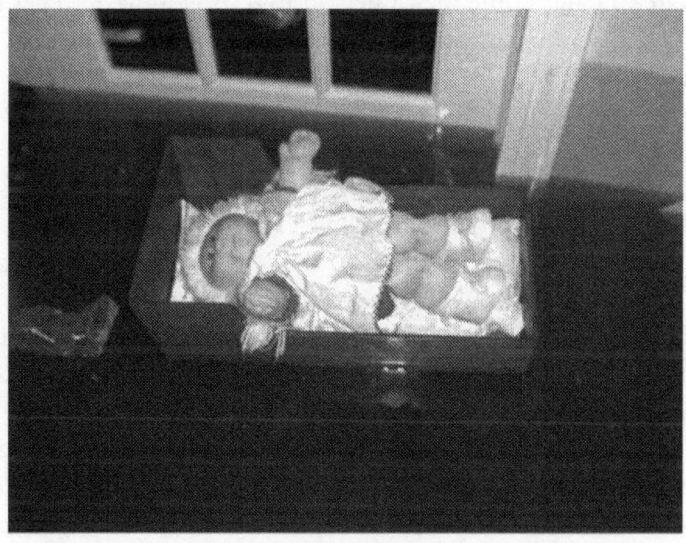

Water Baby

MIZ MARY, Ninth Ward, New Orleans

I went with a few of my neighbors to stay in a hotel for Hurricane Katrina. My house is old and not in good repair, so I didn't want to stay there in the Ninth Ward. It is better for an older person not to be alone at times like that, anyway.

We were just waking up on Monday morning, when the hotel man came and told us we had to leave. The water was coming up and he couldn't be responsible, he said. He put us out and we started walking as we saw many others headed in the same direction. The water rose up from my knees to my chest. I don't know how far we walked, but it seemed like a long time of steady walking.

We were directed to the Superdome. We stayed there two days with no food or water. Finally someone came and told us we'd have to get on a bus. They handed us some water and a package of peanut butter crackers. I wanted to cry because everyone was being so nice. The crackers tasted delicious and the water soothed my parched throat.

When every one of the seats on the bus was filled, we left New Orleans. I knew we were headed west, 'cause the sun was full in my face as it set. It was good to get out of there. I can tell you that for sure.

The driver asked us some questions and when I told him I was a diabetic and needed dialysis, be brought me to a hospital in a little town in Texas, name of Liberty. The hospital was small and the nurses friendly to me. I had a nice shower and shampoo. With a clean, dry nightgown on was able to eat a little soup and a sandwich. I drank the whole bottle of water.

I had my treatment and the awful headache and nausea I'd been feeling for days left my body. It was replaced with an overwhelming wave of sadness. My old house in Ninth Ward was cut off from the world. No one was slowed into that area, the TV on the wall showed pictures of people walking in that nasty water and houses on the sides, and other people on rooftops while helicopters flew overhead.

Me and my friends had been right to leave. Who in the world would think that the levees, which protected New Orleans, would fail. I could not go home. I saw the mess that we used to call home on my TV set and began crying. I couldn't stop, even when the nurse came and sat on the edge of my bed and patted my hand.

"We is taking good care of you, Miz Mary," she said. "You don't need to cry. You is safe, now."

"I ain't crying for myself," I sobbed. "I have a son and grandson. I don't know if they are alive. I don't know if I want to be. I just don't know."

I broke down and bawled into my pillow so as not to disturb the other sick people down the hall.

"You just give me their names, Miz Mary," the young nurse said. "I'll go on the internet and find them for you."

"Oh, would you do that for me?" I asked with hope in my heart. "Can you let them know that I'm alright, too? I know they're wondering, like I am . . ."

"Sure, I can. I'll tell them where you are and give the phone number of the Nurses' Station here on third floor."

"Phones don't work there." I said. "Even my cell phone quit before the water came up."

"We'll get through, somehow," she assured me. "Gotta go give report so I can go home. I'll go online soon as I get there, Miz Mary."

"God will bless you for it," I softly as she left the room.

I said my prayers and for the first time in seven days I closed my eyes and got a good, natural sleep. No bad dreams. When you give your problems to God, you can rest assured that He'll come through.

Patricia Pietrie

Well I made out pretty good for Katrina. Very good, I'd have to say. We left Crown Point, LA on Sunday morning, on the 28th. The traffic was thick and poked along. Jason, my littlest son slept the whole way. His brother, Gerald, the six-year-old played ABC games with his cousin, Mikey, whose girlfriend and he were packed in the back seat of the truck with the kids and me. It was hot, sweaty and slow. Buddy kept worrying we'd run out of gas before we got to the next station, so we couldn't run the air conditioner. We went to a hotel in Bossier City. My mother-in-law, her boyfriend, Buddy and his son, his sister-in-law and her husband and two kids and Miranda, Rachelle, Mikey and his fiancée, Ina. There was only one room available. People were running from that big storm, I can tell you. All in the only room available. At least the air conditioning worked. Late August is *hot* in Louisiana!

The next morning (Katrina passed), we packed up to head home. Didn't think we would get all the way there. We dodged police, took back roads and even dodged debris all over the road. Not to mention some flooded areas and down power lines. We finally made it home that same night of the 29th at around 8 p.m. We slept in my mother-in-law's living room on the floor, with two kids, of course, no electricity. Hot as hell . . . wanting to rip your skin off.

The next morning was my birthday. I got to go home to Crown Point . . . and see that my trailer was fine. There were trees down over the fence and even one budged up against my back door. But everything was fine. Happy Birthday to me! We still stayed by the in-laws for days in the heat, before finally they was able to get passed the police going into Lafitte, LA, to check on my father-in-law's shrimp boat. They finally retrieved the huge diesel generator off the boat to bring back to the in-laws home and run the refrigerator and one window unit. The window unit was put through the windows of the in-laws bedroom . . . so that means . . . we all crashed in there at night.

Stress was everywhere, every day. Couldn't go home . . . without electricity, it was just too hot. I have small children. We would drive to St. Charles Parish, in Boutte, to go to the store that finally opened up. We would take ice chests with us, to buy groceries to bring all the way back home. I live in Jefferson Parish. We finally got lights on after a few weeks and went back home.

I honestly thought I was going to have a stroke at the age of 25. My mom was in Mississippi and my brother in Texas. The only way to keep in touch over the cell phone was to go to the very top of the Industrial Canal Bridge. Lawrence said he hadn't cried in years, until then . . . cause I was home. They weren't allowed in and they were hearing rumors about all kinds of crime going on near us. None of it was true. We did have to fend for ourself. There was hardly anyone around and no store open. But, I'm alive and my house is fine . . . but the next time, I will leave with my mom.

Power Surge, Bay St. Louis, MS

"Mom, I don't want to go to Grampa's house for the hurricane," Richard said. "He doesn't have a computer."

"It's only for a day or so," Kathy said. "We live in a low area, and there may be a surge with this storm."

"But, Mom," Richard protested. "We got a surge protector."

Miss Kitty

CAT STORY, Bay St. Louis, MS

Olga had just moved to the Manor House Apartments after being on the waiting list forever. Elderly and widowed, she planned to live out her "golden years" with someone else mowing the lawn and fixing the plumbing. Her children were all married and far away, raising families of there own. Olga enjoyed her independence. She attended the Senior Center, where she took part in field trips, did Yoga lessons, learned crafts and simply enjoyed socializing with others her age.

When Hurricane Katrina filled the Gulf of Mexico, her children started calling her to come to them. After thinking it over, she called her daughter and let her know that she would not stay in the apartment alone, although it was on a cliff overlooking the Bay.

Tall and willowy, with curly silver hair, Olga had the regal bearing most older nurses possess. Her bright blue eye sparkled behind thick glasses. The only makeup she wore was Chap Stick with moisturizer and SPF 15. She put on dark slacks and a short sleeved shirt. It was summer, so she wore peds with her orthopedic oxfords instead of stockings. Her nurse's watch, with oversized face and numbers, rode upon her left wrist with a bright red watchband. It was the only swatch of color on her person.

She put a change of underwear and toothbrush and toothpaste in a bag. She put down food and water for her cat, enough to last a few days. She scrunched down and ruffled the fur behind Kitty's ears.

"You be good, Kitty. I'll be back," Olga said, closing and locking her apartment door. She got into her car and drove to the Senior Citizens Center.

Olga was assigned to a patient with COPD. Thin and bird-like, Alicia Mae Thompson grabbed onto Olga. Her black eyes were dull with worry, and her dark skin had a grayish pallor. Alicia's breath came in short, gasping gulps.

Olga realized this little lady's anxiety and did here best to calm her. Talking quietly, she learned of Alicia's panic attacks. When you can't breathe, it's really scary.

Getting to know her patient's needs and helping Alicia Mae with breathing treatments and oxygen, Olga was kept quite busy. Better than sitting home alone watching the storm come closer and closer. Olga thought about her cat, and hoped Kitty was doing okay.

Sunday night was quite comfortable in the Senior Center. A large generator was on stand-by in case the electricity went out. Cases of bottled water and canned goods lined the walls of the kitchen. The fold-up Camp Cot was not the greatest, but was better than nothing.

The Administrator of the Center was a large woman with a loud voice. Olga was certain the woman's heart was just a big as the rest of her as she watched her go room to room, making certain everyone was alright and had whatever they needed. The Administrator checked Alicia Mae and once again told Olga how grateful she was for her expert assistance.

Before dawn the next morning, the Coast Guard came to advise moving to higher ground. They helped find transportation and move the people inland. A thirty-five foot wave had been spotted in the Gulf, headed right for Bay St. Louis. The sick people and their care-givers were loaded onto a bus, as well as in several vans, and sent to Kiln Middle School, well inland. Olga left her old blue Nova sitting in the parking lot as she rode the bus with her patient.

The wind had begun to blow in gusts that rocked the bus Olga and Alicia Mae rode in. A few feeder bands in advance of the storm splattered a mixture of rain and leaves as the group huddled into the front door of the building. It was now very cramped situation. The shelter where they were taken was about eighteen miles inland. The school had been recently built, so was considered structurally secure.

The wind had begun to blow in gusts up to 100 mph. There were many people already there, and Olga's group found places where they could, intermingling with the people who had come to the shelter earlier.

Olga and her patient found a good spot in the school gym with an electric plug, set up Alicia Mae's breathing equipment and made themselves a nest. The quilts they'd brought from the Center helped as they settled on the hardwood floor.

The storm began in earnest while they chatted, played cards and read books. The Center had sent water and food along with their people. So Olga made certain that her patient ate something before taking her medicine. She gave Alicia a breathing treatment just before they lost power.

The wind roared around and ripped shingles off the roof, slammed trees and other flying debris into the building, and altogether made a tremendous racket. Hurricane Katrina was not only a fierce storm, it was a very large one, so took its time banging around, causing more damage than was really necessary for a summer hurricane. Olga began to wonder if it would ever be over. And she worried that her cat would be frightened all alone in the apartment.

Part of the roof went and people from that area were herded into the already crowded gym where Olga and her group were. They pushed into more consolidated areas to make room for the newcomers. Everyone was afraid and worried. This storm was not supposed to be this bad. Nothing should be this bad for this long. It went on and on, nonetheless.

After sleeping on the floor with other people all around her, Olga woke up stiff and sore. Being eighty-two was not a recommendation for camping. She wished for a toothbrush, a comb, a shower and a change of clothes. Alas, no genie came to grant that wish. After awhile, she was afraid to lift her arms for fear of offending her neighbors, cause goodness knows, she could smell *them*.

The group waited to see what would be done with them. They had no transportation of their own, no way to get back to their homes, if any homes were left standing. The food and water was scarce and tempers short. Olga had the clothes on her back and her purse. She'd lost her bag of personal items somewhere along the way. She was twenty-something miles from her home in the Bay, and she was worried about her cat. It was not a good feeling, although she felt blessed to have survived the storm at all.

Her patient was taken to Jackson, MS with the other special needs patients, where they would be cared for in a hospital. Olga stood outside and looked around after Alicia Mae left on the bus. She was awed at the sight.

The trees were naked. Not a leaf or pine needle was left on the broken stumps of limbs. Some pine trees had been twisted and the tops snapped off the trunks. Pecan trees lay on the ground, entire root systems torn from the earth. Debris was strewn across the playground of the school. Unidentifiable items looked like an advertisement not to litter. Pieces of tin roofing were wrapped around the limbs of a mighty live oak tree and someone's doghouse lay upside-down against the front of the building. Olga shook her head in denial that such a thing could happen here.

"I'm driving to Bay St. Louis," a man said. "Does anyone need a ride?"

"I do," Olga said. "Please."

They looked at the destruction along the way. When they got to the I-10 underpass, Olga could see the debris line where the high water had been. It was her first indication that there had been flooding. Her apartment was only a short walk from the beachfront, now she was *really* worried about her cat. The man dodged fallen trees, overturned cars and whole house trailers as they passed down Highway 603 toward the Bay. It looked like a war zone, he said.

At the Center, Olga was grateful to see that her car was still there. She thanked the man, got out and walked around to the front of her car.

OH! OH! There was a big tree limb on the hood, and the windshield was smashed out altogether. When she opened the driver's side door, she saw the seat was covered with broken glass. It took time and energy to wrestle limb off her hood and to clean off the seat enough to spread a plastic bag on it. She got in. Olga felt very tired and wondered if the motor would turn over The car was persnickety at the best of times, and Olga wasn't sure that it would even start. It kicked over with the first try.

Driving around fallen trees and other debris in the streets, she made her way to Second Street Elementary School. That was as close as she could get to the place. Olga got out of the car and started south. In just a few blocks she was able to identify the Dentist office, and knew to turn left at the corner.

It was difficult to get through the piles of debris, but she wiggled this way and that as she forced her way toward the beach. She had her purse around her neck so she could use both hands to help her along.

Now picture a tall, thin white-haired elderly lady clawing her way through the amassed trash and broken lives of many a household. All for the love of a cat.

When the silt build-up began to cover the piles of debris, Olga found it sucking at her shoes, making walking even more difficult. Although the mud looked dried and cracked on the surface, it was still wet under the shell which had been baked by the August sun and heat. It got very hard to pull her feet out of the mess, so Olga found the arm of a sofa and sat there while she pulled them off. All she had was what she had on, so she carefully tied the shoelaces together and put that around her neck with the purse. She could feel her toes squish in the watery mess, but couldn't see what she was stepping in under the mud.

Finally, after an eternity of floundering among the trash left by the wave, she saw the top of the wall of her apartment building complex. When she got to the wall of the apartments, Olga wondered how she was going to get over it. She had no doubt that she would, of course.

As she leaned against the wall catching her breath she heard voices on the other side.

"Hello!" she called. "Hello. Anyone there?"

A man's head appeared over the wall. He was middle aged and had incredibly dark eyes under thick, dark eyebrows. His baldhead was streaked with the grayish mud left by the hurricane. His lips were thin and straight.

"What are you doing here?" he demanded.

"I came to see if my cat is okay," Olga said. "But I don't know how to get over this wall."

"Stay there," he said. "We'll be right over."

True to his word, Olga saw him come around to her side of the wall. With him was a younger man. Thin, with glasses and a baseball cap, he had the same dark eyes as the other.

"Put on your shoes," the young man said. "We'll walk you around. Which apartment is yours?"

"Eleven," Olga said. "I can't wear my shoes in this muck. The mud is pulling them off my feet."

"You don't want to step on a nail or a snake, do you?"

Olga put her shoes on and laced them tightly. The older man reached out a hand to help her to her feet and the younger one walked behind as they went around the wall. The upstairs apartments looked untouched except for where the roof was missing on a few units. The trees were stripped of leaves and smaller branches, and gave a ghostly appearance behind the Southern Mansion effect of the front of the building. Olga saw broken windows and boards peeled off the sides of some of the downstairs apartments. She got to the door of number 11.

"I think I left my keys in my car," she said. "Do you think you can break in?"

"I noticed a sledge hammer across the street, Bo," the older man said. "Right behind where that red truck is upside down on the steps."

"You are so kind to help me," Olga said. "What brings you here?"

"We're looking for our sister," he said. "Maybe you know her, Evelyn Wickette?"

"I'm sorry," Olga said. "I only moved in two weeks ago. I haven't met many people in the complex, just my neighbors on either side."

"Oh," he said. "We heard she evacuated with a group of women, and thought you might know about it, since you're a woman."

"Here's the hammer," Bo said. "Where shall I hit the door?"

"Try the handle," his brother said. "Give it a good swing. Stand back, lady."

The door burst open and Olga got a quick look inside. It was as though it had been in a blender. Everything was swirled around and meshed together and coated with the gray Katrina mud. She put a hand over her mouth to keep from crying out.

"Doesn't look too good for kitty," Bo said. "Do you want me to see if I can find her?"

"Please," Olga gasped. "I just can't go in there now."

Both men went into her apartment. They were gone awhile. Olga could hear one, then the other calling "Here, Kitty, kitty, kitty." softly. She held her breath and sent up a little prayer.

The younger man came out, wiping his hands on his jeans. The older one was right behind him, with a long, limp object dangling from shoulder down to his belt.

"Is this what you want?" he asked, as he placed it in her arms.

Kitty was a longhair, matted with Katrina mud, a combination of salt water, silt and backed up sewerage. In spite of it all, Olga buried her face in the sticky mess and cried for happy. KITTY WAS ALIVE!

Olga and Kitty

Billboard seen on I-12 in Slidell, LA:
Does your yard look like a National Disaster? Stumped?
Call 504 555-1313 for stump removal service

Jane Nye and Tom Wallace, Pass Christian

Jane Nye lost more than a house, a new car and everything she owned. Her youngest child and only son was sent to Vermont with two other cousins so they could attend school. He is a senior in High School. He will not be moving back home again. She is saving for the ticket to go watch him graduate.

As Jane looked forward to sharing band trips, Senior Prom and Invitation-writing (not to mention the nagging to get the "thank you" notes written) and her husband, Tom, looked forward to teaching Tommy his golf tricks and driving. The storm washed it all away, too.

Months of sitting, first in a Motel in Pensacola, then in a friend's house while waiting for a FEMA trailer, and finally getting one placed on their lot ½ block from the beach in the Pass, had taken its toll. The boy couldn't go to school because the bridge had been washed away and his school wouldn't start until maybe next year. He slept in a slot alongside the tiny toilet in the back of the camper assigned to them. It was bleak and depressing just being there.

The landscape looked like a B si-fi idea of a dead planet. All the trees were stripped of limbs and leaves. The pines had twisted in the high winds until they snapped like broken umbrellas. Debris scattered and piled up by the wave brought other people's junk to her house foundation.

You could look out over the gray waves under a winter—cloudy sky and see forever.

A Japanese plum tree stood awkwardly on the edge of the house foundations. Jane started putting items on its bare limbs; Mardi Gras beads bleached by the sun, a Barbie doll, and an old Teddy bear. She called it her Katrina tree. She found a few Christmas Ornaments to add class to her decorations.

The wind blew constantly there on the beachfront, with nothing to stop it. A skinny Mocking bird flew in and perched in the Plum tree. It sang a few notes, then took off looking for a home with more shade.

Tom and Jane Nye looked like they were camping on the moon, only some of the misshapen rubble had a familiar look, like a toilet seat with a jar of preserved figs inside or three bathtubs and 4 Duck-tapped refrigerators awaiting who knew what or when for pick-up.

"Tommy will never come home again," Tom said. "He has chosen to go to a college in Vermont after graduating this spring."

"We just were not ready to looked our youngest child, yet," Jane Nye said. "Sure, we knew he would be going away to college next year. This is too soon, we're not ready for this."

"Well, under the circumstances at the time . . ." Laura's husband said.

"Wait, wait a minute, Hon," Laura said, patting his arm and reaching across the table to Tom. "What do you mean, Tom? How do you really feel about your boy living in Vermont?"

"Cheated," he said, looking down at the tabletop. You could hear the raw emotion in his words. "Abandoned."

"There was no home. No schools. No transportation and the bridge to his school washed away even if his school could open."

"It was impossible for him to stay, I know." Tom lamented. "But if I had known our lives would not be together I would never have let my boy climb up on that truck. He would have gotten through the hard times and been a stronger man for it."

"You mean to sleep in the cubby hole next to the toilet would make him stronger?" Jane Nye laughed without humor. "With his Asthma the Katrina Dust would have had him in the hospital all the time. It was the right thing to do at the time . . . the only thing."

"I am just crushed by the loss," Tom said, emotionally

"You know, Tom, some people lost children to this storm all along the Gulf Coast. At least our son is alive and well." she said.

"But so far away," Tom moaned. "I am very grateful to Chuck and Kathy for taking him as their own. It's important that they are cousins. They've been more then kind . . . . I just wasn't ready to loose him this soon."

Wallace

Boly Kol, Jacksonville, FL
(The rescue of Niny, *again*)

Vi Kol escaped from the killing fields of Cambodia. The Karma Rouge murdered her brother and her husband. Mother of three young boys, she was living with friends in Vietnam. There the spirit of her dead brother came to her at night. He would not let her alone until she agreed to rescue his daughter, Niny (Knee knee) from Cambodia.

The government of Cambodia was in disarray. Young men roamed the countryside, killing whomever they felt like killing. There were many hardships, no aid from the government for anyone. It was a dangerous mission for a woman and child to undertake. Vi sold her jewelry to go get Niny. Vi took her son, Boly and had to appear poor and stupid, while financing her journey and seeking her niece.

It was very hot and sweaty in the jungles there. Many times Vi stopped and asked if a woman with a little girl lived nearby, but she couldn't find her sister in law.

Boly complained of the heat and thirst. He was just a young boy and it was hard for him to walk so far. Vi stopped to buy water at a house in a clearing of the dense jungle. She asked if there was a woman with a small girl child living nearby.

"There used to be, but the woman got married and moved away," the old lady said.

Vi's heart felt so heavy, she was running out of courage to continue her quest. "Do you know her new married name?" she asked.

"No, she did not tell me," the old lady said. "You might ask her mother, who lives up that path and to the right of the pond there. Ni left the children with her when she went."

Vi and Boly thanked the old lady and walked up the path into more jungle. Bamboo grew so thick it was almost higher than a house. The insects were drawn to their hot, sweaty bodies and feasted there as they walked along, looking for the path to the right.

They almost passed it by it was so overgrown with disuse. Skirting around the little lake Vi saw the bamboo hut. Three little girls sat around a rice bowl in the packed dirt yard, eating with their fingers.

"Which one of you is Niny Ta?" Aunt Vi asked.

Three pair of dark brown eyes looked up through long dark hair. Their little faces were pinched with hunger and malnutrition. Vi's heart felt like a big hand was squeezing it. Her brother's little girl stood up.

"I am Niny," she said. "Who are you?'

"I am your father's sister, and this is your cousin, Boly," Aunt Vi said. "We would like to talk with your grandmother."

Niny ran lightly up the steps to the thatched hut. Soon she stood in the doorway, leading a withered old lady by the hand. She said something in the dialect of the district and pointed at the mother and son standing in the yard.

"Welcome," Yeah said. "Come in and refresh yourselves. Welcome to my home."

Steppping out of their outside shoes, mother and son entered. The house was very poor and sparsely furnished with several pallets rolled against the walls. There was no electricity or running water here. Boly looked on with big dark eyes as his cousin brought mats for he and his mother to sit on the floor. Yeah offered them water she dipped from a bucket with a cup.

Aunt Vi and Boly drank the water and thanked the old lady.

"Yeah," Aunt Vi began. "I have come to take Niny back with me. The spirit of my dead brother came to me in a dream and told me I must do this thing."

"Did he tell you she has a little sister? One only a year and a half old?" Yeah asked.

"No mention of anyone except Niny was made," Aunt Vi said. "Of course we will take both girls. I know how hard it must be for one so old to have the burden of taking care of young children."

"It is indeed a burden, as the rice grows scarce. I have no clothing for the little ones, and the winds will soon blow colder," the old lady said, with eyes downcast. "I do what I can, but there is no help."

"I will give you help now, and again when I get to Thailand," Aunt Vi said. "You have taken care of the girls a long time without help and it is only right."

Aunt Vi gave the old lady money which would be enough to keep the family fed and clothed for a year to come.

"I will help my cousin on the trip," Boly said. "It is a long way to walk, but I'm a big boy and I can carry her piggy back so she won't get tired."

"God will bless you, boy," Yeah said.

In the end, the little one would not stop her loud crying when the journey began. It was too dangerous to travel with a loud wailing child. It would draw the attention of the marauding bands of killers still at large in the countryside. A quiet child could hide and not be found, perhaps. They had to take the little sister back to the grandmother.

It was a long dangerous way to Thailand. Some of the time they *did* have to hide and keep quiet as they witnessed terrible atrocities committed upon others. Boly was true to his word and helped carry Niny sometimes when she was too weary to walk. The cousins came to love each other as they survived the rugged terrain, danger, heat and insects to escape.

Of course they made it, because they are both living in America today!

Baby Niny

Teddy, Niny, Baby Ziena and I walked the block and a half to the beach, because we heard you could get through on the cell phones there. Pawpaw couldn't go because his legs were vastly swollen and very painful. When we got in the middle of the block, we had to walk up on the porch of a house blocking the street, then jump down on the other side to continue walking.

It was a wonderfully bright sunny day, and the water sparkled like diamonds on the wavelets out in the Gulf of Mexico. As we neared the end of the street, I gasped. There were no houses. All of them were just *gone*! The only traces left were steps, period. Five on the right side and six on the left had been swept away by the wave. Just gone!

As we stood staring in astonishment at the total absence of humanity, my cell phone chirped. I took it out of my pocket with trembling hands. Then I couldn't read the text message, cause I'd lost my glasses. Niny read it for me. It was from Ellen Dodge, my niece in Orange Grove, MS. Niny texed everyone on our calling list to let thrm know we were all alive.

James, my grandson in South Carolina, texed me back, saying his family were so glad we were safe and they had been praying for us.

Boly and his friend, Roman arrived the next day. It was unusual to see anything moving down the street, so when the sleek RV pulled into our drive with gas cans strapped to the top we were awed, to say the least.

Boly was the first to jump out of the car from the driver's seat. He looked like an Asian angel to me. His short, stocky statue, topped by a thatch of thick black hair over a big smile was the best thing we'd seen in days.

"Hot Damn, you got a mess in Mississippi!" he exclaimed. "Got your message. I tried to phone you back, but got nothing."

Roman unfolded his lanky self our of the passenger side of the car and yelled "Hello, everyone." in his cute Russian accent. His suave good looks and European charm spilled out all over the place in this muddy, storm-ravaged environment.

We learned that Aunt Vi, Bolika and Bolina (Niny's other two cousins in Jacksonville, FL.) had collected money for the gas and food, water, ice and other portables. All were very welcome. Boly and Teddy cooked on the grill on the patio, while Roman charmed us with stories of the adventures on the trip.

After dinner, the young people walked down to the beachfront. As a frequent visitor, Boly was also flabbergasted over the total absence of houses.

"Where the f—k did they go? Are they out in the Gulf of Mexico? Maybe there's whole f—in houses in the shipping channel." he said. "You d—n lucky to be alive, you know?"

Roman was astonished to note the two story brick movie theater was gone from the corner by the beach. "We got good snowballs there last week." He also said how lucky we were to be alive.

"I gotta bring you back to Mama," Boly told Niny. "She said you come tomorrow, so get your s—t together and be ready first thing in the morning."

'No, I . . ." Niny began, but Boly cut her off. "I can't f—in go home unless I got you with me," he insisted. "You know how stubborn that woman can be."

"There's nothing for you here but misery, Baby," Teddy said. "You take Mom and Ziena and go. This isn't a good place for y'all right now."

"Right!" Boly said. "You ain't even got flush toilets or f—in running water here. Anyhow, Mama wants y'all there so she'll know you are safe. She'll f—in kill me if I go home without you."

"Alright," Niny agreed. "We can get ready tonight and leave first thing in the morning."

When they returned from their walk, they told me and Pawpaw. I didn't want to leave him but he insisted. Teddy said he would take good care of Pawpaw while I was away. I looked at the mess the house was in and knew it was not a good place for the baby. Boly was very persuasive, as well.

We packed the few clothes we had, along with toothbrushes and went to sleep. The next morning we packed our stuff in the car and left. Teddy and Pawpaw stood on the front porch and waved as Boly turned out the driveway and headed for Florida.

The back seat was a bit crowded with Ziena's baby seat in the middle. Niny and I sat on either side of her and looked out our windows. It was a mess out there, mile after mile. Boly and Roman pointed out interesting devastation points they'd noted on the journey in.

After we crossed the bridges on the other side of Mobile and Pensacola, Boly and Roman began talking to each other, Two-year-old Ziena went to sleep clutching 'Puppy', with thumb in mouth.

After ten hours of driving, we pulled into the driveway of Bolika, Boly's youngest brother. The whole family and many friends were there to make us welcome. Aunt Vi had a wonderful spread of Asian food (She'd made some of Niny's favorites).

Boly smiled at his Mama. "I rescued Niny again, Mama." He said, "but this time I brought a few extras, too."

Yankee Intervention

"My God! Look at the size of that thing!" Chuck exclaimed As he and his wife, Kathy watched the satellite pictures of Hurricane Katrina on their TV set in their home in Fairfax, Vermont. "It fills the entire Gulf of Mexico!"

"Did your Mom and Dad get out?" Kathy asked. She walked over and sat on the arm of her husband's chair, put her arm on his shoulder, knowing how he must dread watching this Natural Disaster approach his hometown down south. "Are Kathy, Lex and them safe? Where is Laura?"

"Mom called that they're on the road to Pensacola, Florida. Kathy had son, Trey, siphon enough gas from the Mopar to fill their tank so they could get out. Laura is at her boyfriend's trailer in the Kiln. Her daughter is with her. They'll be safe from the storm surge, I think." Chuck said. He stroked the hand, which lay on his shoulder, without taking his eyes from the TV screen.

"It's really big. I don't care what category they name it. This is going to be bad for a LOT of people."

On Monday, the screen was filled with reports of New Orleans levee breaking. It showed pictures of the waters rising and people being rescued from cars, rooftops and reporters standing around in yellow parkers talking about devastation and death everywhere.

There was little or no reports of Bay St. Louis, Mississippi. The wave which came in with the monster storm was widespread and pushed waters inland through the many rivers and bayous which feed into the Gulf, but no actual report was complete. It was said that Bay St. Louis, Pass Christian and Waveland were wiped off the map. Everyone there was thought to be dead.

The media was focused on the City of New Orleans where the levees had broken and the flooding was the biggest story around. The Red Cross didn't know anything. They said they would get back to Chuck when he called, but he knew better. They were swamped and over their heads in calls and didn't know where to begin looking for the answers.

As the news went on and on through the next day and night about the extent of the damage, Kathy and Chuck went to the priest at their church who contacted the other denominations around town. They rented a large Big Rider truck and began packing it with donations from the multiple congregations.

Kathy sorted shoes and socks and packed them together according to sizes. She got together feminine products. Manual can openers, matches, tarps, diapers and dog food.

Jennifer, her 13-year-old daughter collected all of her stuffed animals, washed and fluffed each one and packed them to give to the children of the storm. She bought coloring books and crayons and paints with her own saved allowance cash, and put them together in gallon plastic zipped bags for the children. She also took all of her pre-teen books and packed them to send.

"No electricity, no TV. No video games or cartoons," Jen said. "Kids need something to do."

Neighbors from as far away as 60 miles came and brought stuff they thought people could use. Food, blankets, cleaning products, paper products; anything the hurricane victims could use.

The school system sent permission slips for any child who wanted to come to the schools there. They could come back with Chuck.

It took three days to sort, pack and load the truck. Chuck and his teen-aged son, Chris, would drive down the entire Eastern Seaboard and into the middle of the arc forming America's southern most seacoast.

On the first leg of the journey, Chuck drove straight down to Charleston, SC. His mother and dad were staying with his brother who is a lawyer and had a large house. David prepared legal forms for guardianship for Chuck to take with him in case any did want to send their children to Vermont to stay while the storm damaged schools and homes were repaired.

After much hugging and tears passed just into being glad they were able to be together again, Chuck went to bed and slept 22 hours straight. The first real sleep he'd had since the Storm had started to head for his hometown.

"Thank goodness we got all those cans of diesel fuel before we left home, dad," Chris said. The flashing signs on I-10 began warning of "*No gas beyond Tallahassee*"

"I wonder why the gas companies do that Dad?" Chris was really concerned, by his tone of voice. "All the folks who want to go help the storm victims have to raise even *more* just to deliver the stuff. Why don't the gas companies contribute too, instead of getting rich off other people's miseries?"

"God knows, son," Chuck said with the simple honesty he had raised his kids upon. "And *He* doesn't sleep." Through Pensacola, the flashing signs said "NO GAS". Across bridges and through a tunnel and they drove through the city of Mobile, Alabama. After that the signs began to show stripping. Pine trees twisted and snapped. Mighty oaks were stripped of all save the major branches, pecan trees were blown over like toy soldiers. A large shrimp boat was up on dry land between rivers in Pascagoula, Mississippi.

The trees and roadside signs were more and more deeply ruined as the Rider van passed through Webberville, Biloxi, Gulfport, Pass Christian, and Diamondhead and came to EXIT 13. Highway 603 to Bay St Louis/ Picayune. That was when it really hit the men in the truck they weren't in Kansas anymore. There was a Military Stop point, unmanned, so they didn't stop.

The Exit went down, then under the interstate. When Chuck looked in his rearview mirror, he could see the high water mark along the earthworks around the interstate. It ended on a level with the roadway overhead. The once busy intersection where they'd been a few large gas stations and a hotel with restaurant was now littered with every form of debris imaginable. Plastic bags, parts of houses, trailers, cars, boats and bent tin roofing littered both sides of Hwy 603 and filled the median, as well. It looked as though the debris had been bush hogged off the road. It continued to become bleaker as they ventured closer to the coast. The trees were bare of even one leaf or pine needle. The tops of some of the trees had simply twisted off due to the winds. There was a nice-looking speedboat in the branches of a large live oak tree, at least fourteen feet above the ground.

The corner of Hwy 603 and Hwy 90 was having traffic directed by young men in Army greens. Chuck and Chris saw the beginnings of Katrina Tent City at the K-Mart. There were a lot of people in the parking lot. Some stood in lines for bottled water and ice. Some stepped in and out of the stores, Radio Shack, K-Mart, Cato and The Tobacco Shack, with arms full of stock. It was obvious that the water had gone through the buildings and Chuck had to smile when he saw a man carry out a big TV set.

There was nothing to protect these stores. The windows had all been blown out completely and the National Guardsmen had their hands full trying to keep order in the long, winding lines of hot, thirsty people waiting, Many stores and businesses along Highway 90 that were completely crushed. Some still stood, but appeared gutted by the wave that had flowed through. Inns and motels were roofless or had missing walls. The county Library was sad, having books set out in piles on the entry.

When the Big Ryder turned onto Dunbar Ave. it really hit Chuck the hardest. Until then, both had been speechless. Now Chris sucked in his breath and hissed, "my God, Dad. Look at that!"

That being the neighborhood where Chuck had grown up and lived until he got married and moved north. The once beautiful, stately old homes along the Avenue were in various forms of devastation. Tin roofs peeled back like sardine cans, shingle roofs totally gone. Clothing, mattresses, refrigerators, stoves, bathtubs, commodes, cars, trucks, boats and doghouses were strewn around the lawns and hanging from the trees. There had been deep water here, looked like. I passed my Mom's house and hardly recognized the classic ranch-style brick we'd helped her move into just two weeks ago.

Around the corner his sister's two story wood frame still stood. As they drove up, his brother-in-law, Lex came out of the front door carrying a limp piece of sheet rock and some unidentifiable debris. He dropped it outside the fence where heaps were growing. Brushing his hands off on his cut-off jeans he shook hands with Chuck, then threw an arm around his shoulders and gave him a big hug.

Kathy and Richard came running out the open front door and walk, through the picket fence, parts of which was left standing in places.

"Chuck, Chris!" Kathy yelled. "Welcome to my nightmare. Glad you could get through, honey, do you want some lemonade? food? a beer?"

"I'd like a beer, Aunt Kathy," Chris said.

"Not for four more years, little nephew," Les said. "The Barq's is good, though. It's our local root beer."

"Com'mon, Chris," Richard said. "I'll show you where we keep the cooler and stuff. Want a MRE?"

"What's that?" Chris asked, as the boys went around the side of the house toward the garage.

The high-water mark in the house was eleven feet up, into the bottom of the second floor of the house. Lex and Kathy were mucking the house out, taking everything down to the frame, then cleaning and purifying that with bleach water and strong commercial cleaner to get rid of the black mold. Carpet, furniture, appliances, beds, clothing, insulation, books, paintings and photos were stacked in piles ready to go out. Anything the water had touched had to be gotten rid of. Everything was dumped over the fence awaiting the corps of Engineers clean up crew.

All Chuck could do was hold his little sister and cry at first.

"Hay, Dad," Chris called down from upstairs. "Come see Richard's room. It's got a skylight . . . now."

Kathy said, "It's to good to have ya'll here, Chuck. Laura will be here soon. She had to work today."

"Did you get a chance to talk with her about sending JJ up north with us?" Chuck asked. "This is no environment for a little kid."

"Nor a big one, either." Lex said. "We plan to send Richard up with ya'll, since the schools won't open here before November. We hope to get the house mucked out, at least, before we have to go back to teaching."

"Big ones welcome, too," Chuck assured his brother-in-law.

"Dad, can Richard come help us give out the stuff we brought?" Chris asked. "I saw all those people in the parking lot at Winn Dixie when we turned onto Dunbar Ave. Maybe we can take the truck there and give out the things we brought?'

"Good idea," Chuck said. "Will it be alright with you if he comes?"

"Wish we could help, as well," Lex said, putting his arm around his wife's shoulders. "Gotta' keep working as long as it's daylight, though. If we don't get rid of the water-soaked sheetrock and insulation it will start to grow Black Mold."

People crowded around the back of the van and accepted the items Chris, Chuck and Richard handed out. They were very appreciative. Chris was blessed so many times, he's assured of going to heaven when he dies. In fact, he gave away his very own sleeping bag to a kid who looked like he needed it more.

Kathy had been busy getting together a bag for Richard's journey in a plastic bag, called a Cajun suitcase locally. A change of underpants, another pair of shorts and a t-shirt and two pair of socks. That, and his toothbrush, underarm deodorant and a comb was all he had.

Laura drove up and jumped out of the pickup before it was completely stopped. She ran to her big brother and threw her arms around his neck. She cried for happy to see him. Her nine-year-old daughter was a little slower and shyer about leaving the cab of the truck. She held a Cajun suitcase and a few books to her thin chest.

"Hi, JJ," Chuck said. "We're going to visit my daughter Jenny and she will let you ride her horses if you want."

"She's got horses?" JJ's eyes lit up. "I *love* horses."

Chuck got all the papers filled out and signed by the parents. On the trip back to his home, he would stop in Pensacola and pick up another child, Tommy.

As Chuck drove out of his battered hometown with a niece and nephew, he felt guilty leaving it in such disarray. Deep guilt. All the work to be done in town, family and friends needing assistance, and he wasn't able to stay and help. The truck opened from the cab to the back with a sliding door. The kids had dome lights, chairs, food, drink, books, and colors to keep them busy on the ride. Chuck felt like he was transporting aliens.

They spent the night in the motel with Aunt Jane and Uncle Tom. Tommy left with them in the morning. They spent the night at David's in Charleston. Amie made a big fuss over all the children. She'd always been very close to JJ and Richard, since they all lived in the same neighborhood.

As they drove up the I-95, Chuck stopped in Dillon, SC where his cousin, Zee, managed a Shoney's. She'd gotten in touch with him at David's and asked him to stop by and have some lunch on her. What he didn't know was that her crew had been working since the wee small hours cooking up special treats for the children's trip. She was happy to be able to help in whatever way she could.

The day after they got to Fairfax, VT. the children all started school. They had a meeting with teachers and councilors, were given backpacks and school supplies and free lunches for the school year.

THE NEW OLD TIME CHAUTAUGUA

A traveling vaudeville show came to the depot today.
With Marching bands, children clapped hands,
And old one tapped their toes.

Then under awnings, tables set up
With most wondrous stuff.
Free workshops of magic and juggling
Quilting, gossiping and such.
And the children all had their faces painted!

Then onto the lawn, with chairs all in front,
Came the colorful Marching Band-slash-
Chamber Orchestra.
Such happy tunes,
We laughed like loons
At the Quaint way they gadded about.

On costumes outrageous
However courageous,
The troupe acted a live show.
Smiles, laughter and applause were . . .

. . . so strange in this place torn apart.
Look at the town,
Trees and rubble on the ground
Most of us sleep in a tin can on our front lawns . . . Now.

Boys run from behind a black screen,
Red shirts, black pants and no shoes
(Couldn't be *our* kids who all wear Nike and Reeboks).

But, then WOAH!
The boys are going so slowly and look at those facial expressions.
Bursting laughter as the audience realizes
They're running *slo-mo!* you hadda' been there, I tell ya!

Jugglers, musicians
Mystical Magic Makers
Tap dancers and dueling brass
Spoon tappers, rappers,
And a man dancing his weight away.

What a wonderful gift for the Bay.
Flying Karmazov Brothers
Juggling 21 balls at once with assistance from his super son.

The folk singer, Faith, was 90
Her continence sunny,
Her tunes funny.
The style show was classy,
The tap dancer sassy,
But Dusty Rhodes stole my heart away
She sang, "Let's Put a Cowgirl in the White House vote-a-lay-dee, vote-a-lay-dee, vote a lady!"

I never laughed so hard since August 29th, 2005—

St. Rose de Lama Choir
Led by Alfrazier
Gave choral praise to God
For bringing us together in his love.

Comedians, sword fighters,
Jugglers and magicians,
Not to mention a well-choreographed Ninja Fight.
All to astound and amuse
In the old Vaudeville way
Got us out of our can-de-minims,
Gathered together,
To laugh and be happy for a day.

The troupe invited us to eats
And served homemade treats
Baked in a *real* oven
Like macaroni, Dirty rice and cookies.
"Come eat with us.
Welcome all."
On the lawn of the Depot in the Bay.

Debby Du

Hi, Debby

This is an actual record of the e-mails received by Debbie Nye Milligan regarding the massive storm of the Mississippi Gulf Coast She and her family had been visiting just weeks before the storm. We had all attended a party at Lex and Kathy Mauffray's home in Bay St. Louis where we celebrated her visit.

Of course, we were glad to know they'd made it home safe, but I can only imagine the distress she must have gone through until she found that every one of her 'Colonial' family members had survived. Since I was out of the loop at this point, what with my desktop going under water and my laptop hibernating, I couldn't personally get online.

Correspondence from the Internet

Compiled by Debbie Nye Milligan, Widdington, Morpeth
Northumberland, England

Hi Debbie,

Dee and Pete finally left on Sunday afternoon and is with Mike, etc. in Houston. Cell phones are working, because Dad and I have talked with Mike. Do you need his number? Aunt Jane and Aunt Evelyn went to Pensacola, FL. Cathy and Lex stayed at his dad's house behind St. Stanislaus. It is gone now but they are somehow O.K. Have not heard about Aunt Lucy. She stayed at home last we heard.

Of course, you know that dad is with me, but he is eager to see what he has left. Aunt Patty is with Cindy. Janey is on her way to see what she has left in Waveland. But from what we have seen and heard there is nothing there. Cindy gave me a website *www.wlbt.com.* Look at the third trip to the coast and you can probably figure it out. Have not heard from my mom, but one of her sisters called Aimee and told her everyone was O.K., just lots of water in houses. Any more info and I will let you know.

—Original Message—
From: "Deborah N. Milligan"
Sent: Sep 1, 2005 3:12 AM

Alicia, this is Debbie in England, have you all gotten through the bad weather Katrina caused and have you heard anything of the family? I am hoping Mom & Dad left for Texas with Mike & Roxie's families but we haven't heard from anyone. I am hoping Aunt Jane, Aunt Lucy and all the Bay Family got out before she hit. Any news would be a relief if you have any. Love Debbie XXXX

*   *   *

Debbie,

Everyone is OK. The only people we have not heard from is Robert Baker, Laura Cox and Roxie, but I am sure Roxie left and is fine. Your Mom and Dad did go with Mike. I don't know how anyone's homes faired but it is a nightmare in both Louisiana and Mississippi. I don't believe my sister Jane has a house anymore, if you can get to *www.wlbt.com* and look at the 3rd. pass over the Gulf you will see Bay St. Louis and Waveland. We didn't get anything here except higher Gas Prices. If you have any other questions I will try to answer as best I can or find the answers for ya. Miss you all very much, but glad you are home safe.

Love, Cindy

On Thu Sep 1 8:55, 'Deborah N. Milligan' sent:

Cindy, did ya'll get any of Katrina's weather? Did ya'll come through all of it okay? I don't have any news of anyone and I have been wracking my brains to remember who lives where and trying to find emails to get in touch to see if anyone knows how the Family has faired. Mom told me Mike & Roxie were both taking their Campers to Texas before Katrina hit, but as far as I know Mom & Dad were going to stay at Mike's house. I am hoping they decided to go with Mike after all. Do you have any news of any of the Louisiana and Mississippi Family that you could pass on to us? Loves Debs XXXX

* * *

Debbie, everybody is fine, but they're scattered. They're all safe, though. Dee went with Michael and his family to Houston, Roxanne went to Shreveport, Lawrence and Tricia went with their in-laws, Amie and my mom and their crews are in Pensacola, Billy has been staying with Alicia in Atlanta. Patty and Jane are . . . shit, I forgot, but they're okay! Ellen, Kathy and Lucy all chose to ride out the storm and all are okay. I don't remember where Teddy and Robert went, but they're fine. Karen's house in Louisiana got looted but she barricaded it up, nobody was there when it happened.

Everybody has food, clothes, water and shelter, some even have electricity (Ellen has a generator). Amie and Kathy and my mom all lost their houses. I'm so sorry I didn't email you sooner, but it's been crazy here! I've got friends staying in the house and their family isn't doing as well as ours (they live in the country and got robbed at gunpoint for all their food and water). Mom and dad and Tommy are coming to live with me until FEMA can give them a trailer or something to live in on their property.

My mom was going to give me her email password so I could find your address and let you know that your folks and everyone else are ok, but you beat her to it. Whew. It's been hectic, but I'm so glad everybody's fine. The family network has kicked in and everybody's been accounted for and has a place to live. :)

Love,
Lindsay

>From: "Deborah N. Milligan"
>
>Lindsay, this is Debbie in England. Have you come through Katrina's storms
>okay and have you any news of the family? Did your mom and the rest of the
>Bay family get out in time? I have no news of anyone and I have had to hunt
>through old printed emails to find someone who hopefully was out of the way
>and able to give me news. Please let me know any news you have. Love Debbie
>XXXX

* * *

Hi, you are so welcome.

Updates: Aunt Lucy somehow text messaged by cell phone to say the they are at home but ok. Who they are we don't know. Aunt Evelyn is on her way to S. Carolina with David. Mike is at work. Aunt Patty's daughter Jane brought Matthew up to Cindy's and then went to Waveland to find absolutely nothing left of her home. Matthew is now enrolled at school in North Carolina. I believe Aunt Jane is still in Pensacola. We were going to leave this morning to go down to the Bay, but decided against it for a few weeks. #1 the gas crisis that is going on and #2 we are not ready for the boys to see the decomposing bodies that are still down there. Aimee's husband went yesterday and he said it was pretty bad. We are all frustrated that we cannot do anything right now. All we can do is sit back and watch. Dad is trying to come to terms that he may not be able to live down there anymore. Aunt Patty and I are trying to get him to stay here with me. We are already going to have his mail or what's left of it moved up here. In a way, he still wants to see what he does have left. He is with us knowing that there is a gas crisis right now and does not want to pay a fortune for gas or get stuck at a gas station with no fuel. I will tell everyone that you all are thinking and praying for them and I am sure that they do appreciate it. Will send more info soon. If you need to call me by phone.

Love ya
Alicia

—Original Message—
From: "Deborah N. Milligan"
Sent: Sep 1, 2005 12:48 PM

Thank you so much! We could only hope and the news on telly is so horrible that we were scared silly! I just got a new pc and it took me ages to find any emails of people that wouldn't have been smack dab in the middle of it all. Thank the sweet lord that Aunt Jane always sends her emails to a dozen or so people at one time and that some are so cute that I print them out. Give everyone our love and tell them they are in our thoughts and prayers at this time. I will check out that web site when I have let all the girls know what news I got. I tried Roxie's mobile and couldn't seem to get through from England. I would like to try Mike's if you can send it. Thanks again, love you all XXXX

*   *   *

Yes, Debbie if you don't mind. I would love to see their emails as well. And please feel free to share mine with them too. Don't know about Mike's pool, but Jane called and her house is gone, but her boyfriend's house still stands. Needs a new roof and had about 4-5 ft. of water in the house. The pool in his back yard still stands but needs a good cleaning. :)

On Fri Sep 2 13:05, 'Deborah N. Milligan' sent:

Bless your wee cotton socks! I start getting info on how the pets have done and then these kids will find something else they need to know, like whether or not Uncle Mike still has his Pool in the back garden. Not to worry!, it seems everyone is accounted for and that was the main worry! Would you like a copy of the emails that Alicia & Lindsay sent me with news? It is pretty much the same but the details between all ya'll's news is a little different so it might help you to get more information. Luvs XXXX

*   *   *

Just found out this motel we escaped to has internet access so Tom got us a laptop! We're fine, our home probably isn't. We left the cats inside & I pray that they survived. Ellen is going to try to go down to look for us. She stayed in North Gulfport. They had some damage to their home, but it's livable. They have running water, a generator & food & ice. Their biggest problem is trying to find gas. Have only had a brief text message from Lucy saying they were ok & stayed in there home. No other word.

Send me some news, please.
Love, Jane

*   *   *

Thanks, Deb. Talked to Lucy last nite. It was so good to hear her voice. She, Ninny & little Ziena are in Jacksonville with Ninny's family. She had about 3ft water in her home. Rob & his wife spent the hurricane clinging to their roof but, thank God, they survived! Aunt Amie & Kathy homes were both under water. They have gone to Charleston with David. They finally had a call from Laura & she & JJ are both fine. She's staying at the hospital in Gulfport where she works. Ellen finally was able to go by our house yesterday. There is nothing there. Everything from (including) our house south is gone. I hope to get a FEMA trailer in the not to distant future. This motel is nice. We have a small fridge, a microwave, a coffee maker, free continental breakfast, access to a washer & dryer & are walking distance to a couple of restaurants. There are several evacuees here & we share information & resources. We are so much better off than so many others! The biggest problem most of us face is the gas shortage.

"Deborah N. Milligan" wrote:

I have emails from Alicia & Cindy that I will forward to you in case there is a bit news you haven't gotten yet. I spoke to Mike & Tammy. Mike called me from his work place in Houston. The company he works for has an office there (that's why they went) and they put him straight to working in that office.I phoned Tammy's cellphone and she told me that FEMA was there supplying them with clothes, toiletries, hot meals etc. They have Rachelle with them and she will be going in to have the baby by Tuesday if she doesn't go into labour herself meantime. Mom & Dad are with them but I haven't had a chance to chat with them yet. Roxie & Joey are in Meridian? with Joey's Brother Ernie & his family. Pete called me last night and said Lil Lawrence went on a boat with his in-laws and they are all doing well. I don't get the full list of names from people but I don't get missing people reports so I take it that all the kids are accounted for somewhere. Mike and the boys were headed back to Marrero yesterday to check on the houses and pick up what they could salvage and hopfully board up where they could before heading back to Texas again. I was looking at some video and satalite picture links via the web address that's in Alicia & Cindy's emails and could only recognise a small area and couldn't make head nor tails of the rest. The photos covered the path of Katrina but the little box that covered Mom, Mike & Roxie's area would not download! It's great to have you back online! Love Ya'll XXXXX

*   *   *

Hey there:

All is good with the family. Mike called Pete Saturday night after he went to check the situation and recover what he could. I'll give you what I understand third hand from their conversation. He was somewhere near Opelousas when he called in on his way back to Houston and they fared just fine other than a flat tire. Neither his house or Mom and Dad's had any water in it. They were missing some roof tiles and siding but no major damage. Mom's Magnolia tree in the backyard is gone and the siding on the driveway side of the house recieved damage. I think he said Roxie's house got some tree damage and she had left their camper in MS so it is totaled I'm sure. As far as we know, Roxie is still in Meridian at the camp. I will call right now and try to reach them and will ask about Lawrence and his wife and will let you know the minute I know anything.

Can't wait to see pics. Mine are kind of spread in folders throughout my PC but I'll gather some together for you. I'll be in touch soon. Hugs and kisses to you, Keith and the girls and Kian too!

Love from us—
Kim

>
>From: "Deborah N. Milligan"
>Date: 2005/09/05 Mon PM 03:28:48 EDT

>Hello! Finally got a chance to get back on send ya'll a note. Haven't had a chance to ring Mike's cell phone and see how he did when he went back to Marrero or even if they let them in. Have you all heard anything new? I had Irene (Big Lawrence's sister) on the phone from Morpeth asking if I had any news of Lawrence or the kids and their families. Big Lawrence had phoned his mom on Sat before the hurricane and said him & his wife were headed for a hotel but he didn't say which one or where. I told her what I knew about Law & Tricia and that I couldn't get in touch with them just yet to ask if they knew where their dad was but I would let her know as soon as I knew.I am still working on putting the Louisiana photos onto this new PC and will send you some as soon as I can knock the kids off it again. We do have a laptop as well but Keith won't let them hook it up to the Net so none of them want to use it. Tina come home with some Office work so I sent her on it! Catch yas later, gonna work on the pics! Luvs XXXXX

*   *   *

David Cox wrote:

Date: Tue, 06 Sep 2005 16:36:59-0400
From: "David Cox"

Subject: fwd: thank you.

Just wanted to share with you an email I gave to my friends and colleagues who have been concerned about my family, to describe somewhat the situation beyond New Orleans. You already know the details. People in Charleston and my friends near and far have been wonderful.

David S. Cox

Date: Tue, 06 Sep 2005 15:39:47-0400

This email is going to a lot of people. I want to share some first-hand information about the damage from hurricane Katrina. Most importantly, I want to thank each of you. I returned to work today to scores of emails and phone messages expressing concern for my family and offering assistance. I'd prefer to communicate with each of you individually rather than send a broadcast email, but under the circumstances it makes sense.

Everyone in my family is now accounted for, and everyone is fine. Believe me, we are very grateful for that. Amazingly, it took six days for that fact to get confirmed. Communications down there are pretty wrecked. Unfortunately, there are friends of our family in Bay St. Louis who died in the storm.

For some of you who don't quite know exactly where it is, my hometown of Bay St. Louis, MS is roughly between New Orleans and Biloxi. It is the county seat of the county on the state line with Louisiana. It was settled by Bienville in 1699. At about 28 feet, its downtown bluffs are the highest waterfront elevation on the Gulf of Mexico. It is a beautiful little town.

Bay St. Louis suffered a direct hit from Hurricane Camille in 1969, a category 5 storm. Our family lost our house in that storm. The surge from Camille was around 24 feet. I have grown up with the fundamental understanding that hurricanes don't get worse than Camille. I was wrong. Although Katrina's winds backed off somewhat to Category 4, its storm surge was significantly worse, and I imagine meteorologists will study why that was the case. Basically, it was a much larger hurricane, with a very large eye, and it came ashore at an angle and a slow speed which apparently allowed a maximum amount of water to get stacked up ahead of it. Based on the water line at the downtown house where my sister and her family rode out the storm and its known elevation, they estimate the surge at 31 feet.

Consequently, the town is pretty thoroughly devastated. I'm not sure what other word to use. Everything got flooded to some degree. The historic downtown is oriented to the Bay. The combination of the eyewall winds, the surge, and the wave action from the surge destroyed almost everything along the immediate water front. Only the strongest structures on the waterfront, e.g. the dominant Catholic Church—Our Lady of the Gulf—are still standing. I went in the church. It's roof is mostly gone. Parts of the solid brick towers are crumbling. The water went through and swept all of the pews up to the alter. I was amazed. A couple blocks inland, the downtown homes and businesses fared the best, with "only" a couple of feet of water in them. Most of them also have at least some roof or window damage.

In the areas away from the high down town, the flooding was more complete. My mother and sister have homes in the Cedar Point area at an elevation of about 12 feet. Their homes got inundated almost to the crest of the roof. Mom's house also had a wall blown out and a roof partially peeled.

The damage in the smaller towns of Pass Christian and Waveland, which flank Bay St. Louis on either side and which are at somewhat lower elevation, was even more complete. Most homes were simply swept away with nothing left.

Again, all of my family either evacuated completely, or at least evacuated to places that were high. Most who stayed did so with the confidence that if a place was dry in Camille, it would surely not be reached by a surge from this one. Again, that confidence was misplaced, as it turns out.

My mother and stepfather's house is a total loss. Same goes for my sisters. I have uncles, aunts and first cousins in Bay St. Louis, Pass Christian, Waveland, Slidell and greater New Orleans. About a dozen of their homes are lost. And their vehicles.

I went down to there on Wednesday with a van full of supplies and came back with a van full of people. Sadly, what you have heard about a lack of any official response is true. I was all over Hancock County—the passable parts anyway—looking at shelters for one of my sisters. I saw a couple of humvees, and that's about it as far military / national guard type response. I saw plenty of helicopters, none of which seemed to be landing in BSL. It was about 95 degrees and people were running out of water. There was a water drop off in the middle of town, but it was quite a hike. Again, virtually everyone's cars were flooded.

Heading in, Pensacola was the last place with available gas, with two hour lines. Maybe this was part of what hampered official respondents, who knows. Had I not brought ample auxillary tanks, I would have run out of gas. Plenty of people did on I-10. By the way, if you have heard that the storm surge went all the way to I-10, it's true. There was a debris line on the eastbound shoulder.

I don't know when running water will be restored to BSL. There was talk down there, hopefully rumor, that the water and sewer system was badly damaged. That will make life tough indeed for those who are trying to clean up. My sister and brother in law are among those who have already returned to roll up their sleeves and start working on resurrecting their properties. I wanted them to stay with me a bit longer, but they are determined. They purchased a truck here and loaded it up with supplies and headed back yesterday. Unfortunately, I fear that it will take a long time to get the town on its feet.

I have a niece and nephew who will be heading up to my brother's farm in Vermont to begin school. We are told it will be a couple months at least before any school can open on the Mississippi Coast.

My mother and step-father are staying with me indefinitely until we can figure out what to do next. Lydia and Spence are lifting their spirits, and Pam and I are doing well.

So, life goes on. We are just about over the shock of it all now, and are moving forward.

Again, please know how grateful my family and I are to have your thoughts and prayers.

*   *   *

—Original Message—
From: *Deborah N. Milligan*

Wanted to let ya'll know that Rachelle had her baby! Brayden Joseph Duhon was born at 5:45pm yesterday the 6th of September in Houston, Texas. He weighed 6lb 8oz and was 19 inches long. Both Rachelle and Brayden are doing well! Mom said Mike got a hold of the baby and wouldn't give him up. Sounds like my lil Bro is a Proud Grandad!

Mom says they are doing pretty good in Houston. They got some food stamps and all the boys are in school. Mike is working for his company there. Some Texan's from further up brought in some fresh game for them and that made my Dad happy and gave him a job to do.

Roxie says her and Joey are fine in Meridian, Miss. with Joey's brother & family. They have a generator but no hot water so you know who is having a shower by the scream! She has to wash clothes in a tub in the yard and peg them out to dry. Hey! I still peg 'em out! They have applied for food stamps and hope to get them in a week or so. She says Patricia & Gerald are back in Lafitte doing okay but Tricia has to go up on the Lafitte La Rose Highway Bridge to get phone reception to keep in touch. Lawrence and Misty are in Galvaston, Texas with Misty's family and they are doing okay. Roxie says the worst of it all is that she is so far away from her kids and the rest of the family. She can't get reception for her cell phone unless she goes into town, I only got to speak to her when I happened to try her cell as she was taking Joey in to the dentist.

They all are hoping to get back home soon as Jefferson Parish gets Electric, Gas and Water back. They know I have been in touch with Alicia, Cindy, Lindsay and Aunt Jane and thanks to them was able to ease my heart about you all and finally get in touch with my Mom, Dad & all. They send their Love!

We also found out about big Lawrence Whittle and his wife. They are safe, but lost their house and his wife's business in Slidell. His sister here in Morpeth did the same as me and burst into tears when she finally heard he was safe this afternoon.

Our thoughts and good wishes, prayers and especially our Love is sent to you all for I know it was hard for those that endured Katrina and lost so much memories as well as their homes. I myself know only too well how hard for it was for family who lost touch for those long long days till we found you all again. We love you XXXXXX

*   *   *

It appears you get better phone coverage from England—Go figure :) I've been unable to reach my sister Melinda but have left her a couple of voice mails. She did call several days ago and reached Pete, and said they were in Baton Rouge and doing okay). Couldn't get Mike's cell, or Roxie's cell phone last night either. I think a lot of the problem is that the towers here in the US are tied up with so many trying to call family and friends. I keep getting a "lines are busy" message.

Glad Roxie is holding up okay—we've been very worried as Mom told Pete that the state of MS has not been at all helpful. I could handle the washtub laundry and the old clothesline method but cold showers—ouch!! Let me guess, the loudest scream (and lots of cussing) must be Joey right? In this amount of time, they would have been here in Las Vegas a week ago had they headed West. I hope they know now—never, never evacuate to MS for a hurricane. They could be here in sunny (and HOT) Las Vegas on "vacation". We've got warm showers here!

Yep—we got the news about Brayden and Rachelle and are thrilled that they have gotten through that okay. Mom told Pete that Mike was over the moon—proud Grandpa Mike!!!

Very happy that Lawrence and his wife made it out safely. All in all, I guess we can count ourselves in a better state than some families. We've got a pretty thorough head count and for the most part, we at least know how to reach each other and I'm grateful for at least that. Thanks for sharing your news and I'll be doing the same. Just haven't been able to make much contact. Take care—Love from us

>
> From: "Deborah N. Milligan"
> Date: 2005/09/07 Wed PM 02:38:47 EDT
>
> Been on the phone to Roxie! They went into town as Joey needed a tooth pulled so her phone had reception! They doing pretty good considering. They are running a generator, washing clothes in a tub and pegging them out on a line. Hey! I peg mine out on a line! They have to take cold showers and she says you can tell who is showering by the scream! You probably know from mom that Rachelle had her little boy Brayden Joseph Duhon at 5:45pm he weighed 6lb 8oz and was 19 inches. Mom says Mike wouldn't give him up! After I hung up with mom she said the baby crowned so Rachelle didn't need the c-section after all! Big Lawrence and his wife Nicky(?) are safe and well, they had scarpered to Florida. They lost the house and Nicky's business but they are safe! i phoned his sister and she was nearly in tears with relief and kept giggling with happiness. catch Yas Later! XXXXX

*   *   *

Hi Deb:

Mike got a new email address set up for them in Houston so we can keep in touch with them more easily. He asked me to send it on. Please share with those you have addresses for. I managed to keep hold of Aunt Jane's (see cc:) but I know you have a more extensive list.

Hi Aunt Jane:

Regardless of distance apart or time away, please be assured of our continued prayers for the entire family, our many friends, and so many others who have been both directly and indirectly affected by this disaster. You are all on our minds daily and we hope for a speedy recovery and continued safety for all . . . And we send lots of love from Las Vegas.

Take good care.

Sincerely,
Kim and Pete
Jessica and Jimmy Lyons (and Nikolle and Lil Jimmy)
Mandi and Darren Segura (and Shaun Pierre)

*   *   *

Deborah Nye Milligan wrote:

All of you have been in our thoughts and in our prayers through out Katrina's journey. We hope you all have come through her terrible winds and water alive and well. I know we may not hear from you until things begin to get back to normal, but we wanted you all to know how much we love and miss ya'll. We wanted to you to know how much we think about ya'll! Take Care and let us know how ya'll have faired as soon as ya'll have a chance. Sending all our love, Debbie, Keith, Michelle, Bryon, Jamie, Kirsty & Kian XXXXXXX

*   *   *

Izzi and Mike

Izzi and Mike Keiser, Waterbury Center, VT

They came from Waterbury Center, Vermont, almost to the Canadian Border, riding in a big dump truck. No air conditioning and no radio for comfort. Top speed 45 mph and got 12 miles to the gallon of diesel fuel. All the way down the continental USA to the Gulf of Mexico, where cousins were in need.

Hurricane Katrina was 9 months gone, but the scars were as yet unhealed. stands of pine forest stood dead and gray against the blue sky. The salt water had stood long enough to kill the roots. Houses still stood, gutted by the wave and waiting demolition or reconstruction. It was all so unbelievable. It had been almost a year since the disaster and still so much to be done.

A cell phone call put Izzi in touch with cousin Lucy, who was at that moment helping a friend dig out a few items from her home to take back to the FEMA camper she now called home in Pass Christian, Mississippi. Lucy talked them to her own house and was there shortly behind the big dump truck. Cousins hugged and said how well each other looked.

Mike is big and grizzly, like a mountain man. His sandy-colored mass of curly hair was covered with a baseball cap, and his mischievous grin making his blue eyes twinkle, and his lips curled upward in the shadow of his graying beard.

Izzi, his wife, is opposite. She is petite, blonde and looks natural in shorts. Ordinarily, she runs a desk in a large building on top of a hill in Montpelier, but was right at home bunking on an air mattress in the reconstruction site of her cousin's home. (Said cousins still living in a FEMA camper parked in their driveway).

As we drove up the Highway 603 to Rob's land in the country, Mike and Izzi couldn't get over the extent of the destruction still evident here. They kept exclaiming, "I had no idea." "This is unbelievable." "You just don't see this on TV."

Driving into the countryside north of town the trees are dying where salt water stood and soaked to the roots. Thousands of acres of pine trees dead, and debris in the trees show how high the water was: thirty-eight to forty feet in some places fifteen miles inland from the Gulf. Signs of reconstruction stood next to battered abandon homes, side by side. Who when or *if* the owners would ever come back to live?

Rob was clearing out dead and broken trees from the bit of land his in-laws gave he and his wife to build on. Sherida and his four children were still in Texas, where they'd been re-located after their rental home was totally damaged. Mike and Izzi were given the tour of his land as he explained where he was going to build the house, the dog kennels and his work shed. He also showed off his FEMA trailer where they would live until the house could be built.

When Izzi climbed on top of the big dump truck, Mike rolled back the tarp, opened the back end and revealed a treasure of household goods, clothing and "stuff". The Ethan Allen chest of drawers was filled with games his children could play, which was a plus for which he was grateful. His kids grew up in the town of Bay St. Louis, and might find the transition to country a bit difficult. One by one they took the items and placed them in Rob's front yard. Washers, dryers, basins and toilets, cabinets, coffee and coffeemakers, kitchen sinks and lots of lumber.

"I have enough here to build a good house, and then some," Rob said, waving his arms over the contributions assembled in his front yard. "I can't believe the generosity of these people who don't even know us. Okay if I share?"

"A-yeah," Mike said with his Yankee twang. "I don't think you need two kitchen sinks, but it you know someone who can use it . . ."

"My whole construction crew relocated to Texas," Rob said. "When our boss came to ask us to come back, we had to leave our families there until we could find a place for them here. Now the guys will have a way to get their families back home. Thanks, Mike and Izzi. Ya'll are the BEST!"

Mile gave Rob some gas cards to help with the U-Haul to bring his wife and kids home.

It wasn't until his mom, Cousin Lucy, came home from a trip to see her grandsons graduate from High School in South Carolina that she found the check written for Rob and his brother Ted in the refrigerator of her under construction house.

The love and generosity of our Yankee cousins will long be remembered and appreciated by those here on the Coast. We feel as though the government has forgotten us. It's nice to know that our fellow Americans have not.

The Library Book, Bay St. Louis

There are many stories of contributions from churches, corporations and individuals. This is a story of one small contribution which really touched my heart in a very personal way. One thing I have always tried to give my children and grandchildren is the love of reading. Adventure, travel and just opening the pages of a book can have entertainment.

My granddaughter celebrated her third birthday five days after Katrina hit. Her personal bookcase was flooded with salt water mixed with backed up sewerage.

She saw it and exclaimed, "What a MESS!"

We couldn't go to the library together for the longest time, because the wave had hit there, too. When they finally opened, we drove over to get some books to read together. She still remembered the destruction of the storm and the condition of her own books.

"I can't read my books, Grandma. I can't have them because they're all messed up by the hurricane. Daddy had to throw them all away," she said. "I want to get some to read at the library."

When we'd been evacuated to Jacksonville (rescued by Niny's family, but that's another story) I'd found a copy of Ziena's favorite book which she'd checked out of the library most often, "*The Princess and the Potty*". I wanted her to at least have something familiar with her while we were in exile from normalcy.

Now that we'd returned to live in Bay St. Louis again, I've taken Ziena to the library, where she discovered that the children's department was ruined when the water flowed through. A single rectangle box of children's books was all that's left for her to choose from. No more puppet theater, no computer, no 'reading rocker' for Grandma, but saddest of all, not one copy of *Princess and the Potty* was left for her to check out when we visited.

The library was sadly depleted. but planning a wonderful comeback.

As Teddy helped his little daughter down the FEMA trailer steps he handed me four books. We always check out three for her. I looked at him as I took the books. Her personal copy of *The Princess and the Potty* was among them.

"This one is hers." I said, handing it back to him.

"The library doesn't have "*The Princess and the Potty*," Ziena said.

"The hurricane took it away. If I give them mine, I can check it out and other little girls can read it, too."

Ziena wouldn't give it herself. "You do it, Grandma," she said, and hung back, watching to see that I did.

After that we went to the shelf designated as the children's area and found her a small chair to set by my regular one. We read a few books before choosing three to take home.

Miss Sue gave Ziena some special stickers, then we went to read the three book she had chosen to take back to the FEMA trailer she now calls home.

Bleak Beachfront

Volunteer from North Carolina, Jill Hamilton-Anderson

When Hurricane Katrina struck the Gulf Coast in August of two thousand and five, I was employed by the U.S. Government. My title was Education Program Coordinator at Carl Sandburg Home National Historic Site. My husband and I both work and our four-year-old son, Lairs, went to day nursery. He was growing fast and learning a lot and just such a lovable handful of child. We were blessed and knew it.

When Katrina hit the Gulf Coast, Uncle Sam called his Federal workers. As a federal employee, I was pressed into duty of one week in December. I hated to leave my guys, but it was going to be an adventure to see where the most severe storm ever recorded in American History had come ashore.

My job was to hold the 'Stop, Slow' sign to direct traffic as the Corpse of Engineers cleaned debris from the side of streets in the small town of Bay St. Louis, Mississippi. It was cold and damp and I had expected a semi-tropical paradise on the American Riviera. Instead, I inhaled dust and swatted mosquitoes as I stood in the street every day for a week. Enough, already.

I could see the homes of residents. Theirs was a crushing blow. What the water didn't ruin, the winds and tornadoes did. There was not a house anywhere with the whole Gulf Coast that didn't suffer from Hurricane Katrina in some way, shape or form.

The folks were out in their yards, sorting out what they had left. One woman picked up a patchwork quilt out of a big washtub and twisted the corner and on down until she wrung out the whole thing. Then she gently draped it on the tin roof of her carport, which sat on the downed pecan tree on the front lawn, to dry. A man oiled up his kid's bike and sat there, just rolling the back wheel to make sure the rust was out. A little girl placed ornaments in a carnation bush for her Christmas tree.

What hope they all showed. What guts to stick it out when all was just trashed by Mother Nature. What courage to stay, in spite of the fact it *could* happen again next hurricane season. It was *their* town and they would not be pushed out of it.

After a week of forced labor, my friend Mabeleen decided to stay and work. There was a lot to be done, and she had worked in construction at one time, So she jumped on the back of a contractor's truck and took off for Slidell, LA. Later she called to say she has a sweet apartment in Slidell and wanted me to come down and stay when my vacation time came around.

We had a blessed Christmas, Wayne, Lars and me. We had just the right stuff that we each wanted, a nice home and a safe yard for playing. I wondered about the little girl who decorated the Camilla bush. How was her Christmas? Was she living in her house yet? Maybe. How long does it take to rebuild one home? How does a body do it all by himself? He doesn't. He shouldn't have to.

"Earth to Mommy," hubby said. "Come back, come back where ever you are."

"I was thinking of those people in Mississippi, Wayne," I said. "Wondering what Christmas must be like for them this year."

"I know, honey," Wayne said sympathetically. "You take on the worries of the world, woman. You put too much upon yourself."

"Wish I could do more than just wonder, is all," Jill said and smiled at her husband. He understood her better then she understood herself sometimes.

"When is your vacation time due?" he asked. "We can plan for your return trip. Lairs and I had a great old time when you were away last week."

"Man time!" Lairs said, small plump fist in the air. Then he went back to playing with his train set and ignored the grown-ups who were talking so seriously about stuff that he didn't care about.

The month of June was very different in Mississippi than the previous December had been. The heat and dust were choking me even though the air conditioner in the car was pumped up. I noticed the deadfall of the trees before I saw any actual damage. Maybe they'd gotten it all fixed up by now. It had been ten months since the storm struck.

No, there were blue roofs on some of the houses along the Interstate when I crossed the state line from Alabama to Mississippi. There was a large shrimp boat sitting in the marsh grass along the Singing River. The longer I drove, the more damage from the hurricane was noticable. Even ten months after the fact, people were still camping in tents. The Blue Roofs (which were actually tarps held down with strips of wood nailed over the original roof) were becoming tattered and showed gaps where rainwater could do further damage to a home.

Not that there was a snowball's chance of rain, the local weather report was *dry, dry and more dry.* Dust hung over the wetlands along the Interstate as I approached Biloxi. Dead trees leaned against thirsty live ones. It was hard to tell what was dead and what was just dying. What freaky weather for these parts. I hoped people were being careful of fires. It wouldn't take much to send the whole forest up in smoke.

When I arrived at Mabeleen's house in Slidell, I was so tired. It was a long fourteen-hour drive for me. My legs were cramped and my back felt like it had broken somewhere along the way. Furthermore my butt had gone to sleep. I almost fell on the ground with the pain of it's suddenly waking up when I got out of the car.

That night, after we'd talked ourselves silly, I asked Mabeleen which area *she* considered the hardest hit. After all, she was all over the place with the contracting jobs.

"I think the Bay/Waveland area could use the most help," she said after a few moments of deep thought. "Of course, there isn't much for you to do in Waveland, as the storm washed the whole town clean. However, there are many homes in the Bay still standing, waiting for someone to help them get it back together."

"What do I do?" I asked. "Do I just go up and ask folks if they want my help?"

"You go to the County Courthouse and register," she pulled out a map and showed me how to get there from here. "They'll direct you from there. I know lots of volunteers who have come on our site asking how they can be of help. I always send them there."

"Okay," I said with a big yawn. "I'm hoping I wake up in time to get something done tomorrow . . . I mean today." My watch said after midnight. I was really beat.

The people at the makeshift trailer courthouse were very nice. They registered me in and told me that any church would have groups going out to help, just latch onto one.

I remembered one such church that had tents all over both sides. It was on a barren street, which dead-ended in the water. I found out there were a lot of those, from Main Street all the way to the Highway 90 Bridge, which was no longer in use, either.

Finally, I saw the A-frame of the First Presbyterian Church amid even more housing. There were trailers, RV's, tents and a double row of barrack like buildings of wooden framework and parachute material. The pastor said they'd had to build extra bunks for volunteers plus buy a larger hot water heater to accommodate showers for all the workers. He welcomed me and offered me a room with a view, of more rooms.

I had breakfast in the church assembly hall with all the other workers. They were from Presbyterian Churches located in different states across the nation. The foreman was a local woman named Bridget. She was tall, blonde and had a great smile for one so overworked and underpaid. She made up the assignments, figured out how many were needed for each job and tried to suit the crews to the type of work that needed doing. I was sent to a house in town with the youth pastor and three boys from a church in Florence, SC. Bridget took us to the house, introduced us to the elderly lady there, and left us.

Paul, the youth pastor, had two of the boys put up sheetrock in the bathroom, while the other boy painted crown molding and baseboards outside. He painted the walls in the living room and I was assigned the trim. We worked together, with the lady of the house offering water and lemon aide to counter the intense heat.

At lunch the foreman collected us and we were taken back to the church for lunch. The food was healthy and plentiful and the company lively. Everyone had a story to tell about what they'd seen and heard about the hurricane. According to some of the guys, we were the lucky ones because we were working in air conditioning. Some of the houses needing help didn't even have electricity or flush toilets.

The elderly lady was so grateful for the help we gave her. She said how good the paint job looked and how neat the trim was. Best of all, she liked the job done on the bathroom ceiling. It had been sagging and had brownish watermarks where the wind-driven rain had come in through the attic vent. The boys put up the new sheetrock and ceiling tiles and it looked like new.

Each day I got to meet new people and help another home on it's journey to being lived in once again. It did me more good than I can say to see the happy faces of those I was able to help, just the little that I did. There is so much yet to be done before the town is on it's feet again, but I am proud to say, "I helped".

Wal-Mart, Waveland, MS

What would this community have done without Wal-Mart?

There was no place to buy *anything* around here for about forty-five days after the storm. We were so glad to have the boxes of food, clothing, cleaning stuff and personal needs that were sent to us from all over the USA, Not to mention the MRE's the National Guardsmen gave us when they arrived. We didn't think about it for a while. Then, the shopper which had been buried under layers of PTSD came forward. The yearning became so intense one had to drive to Slidell, Louisiana or Gulfport, which was thirty-some miles away. So if said shopper had a car, or could get a ride, it was okay.

The rest of us sat at home, graciously accepting much-needed living items, like water, ice, clothing, shoes, etc., wishing we were *Shopping!*

At last Wal-Mart opened a tent store in the parking lot of the original store. It had flats of items pertinent to our needs. The Styrofoam ice chest went on sale just as our old one fell apart. There was insect repellent of every description, along with nets to wear over the hat to keep the gnats,'no seeums', out of your face. (Of course, the little buggars found a way to sneak in, anyway and get between eyes and glasses and generally drive one *insane*.") There were dishtowels, bath towels toothbrushes, hair combs and lots of sunscreen.

Our local hardware store, Hubbard's, and 84 Lumber opened as soon as possible to meet the needs Wal-Mart couldn't. Between them, we were able to buy materials necessary for the job at hand, rebuilding our towns and communities.

It really felt good to go into Wal-Mart and see the familiar faces and smiles of the old crew. Wal-Mart became the place where you met friends you wondered if they were killed or moved away. It became the focal point of social gathering, like the town wells in the olden days. Women and men alike would stand around and talk, exchanging stories of the storm or ideas of remodeling that old kitchen or adding on a room.

Wal-Mart put out a DVD on Hurricane Katrina, but I am too personally involved to watch so far. I get to a part that hits me hard, and have to leave the room. It was a humdinger, alright. My husband says that if he just hears of someone going to 'pass wind' around here, he's leaving.

Wal Mart may be a big cooperation that serves the whole United States and beyond, but they are hometown to each community they serve. I can tell you first hand, I don't think we would have done as well without them being here in Waveland. It's still the only store in town.

Ted

Teddy's Shower, Bay St. Louis

July 28, 2006. This morning I was jolted from my bed by an enormous clap of thunder and the sound of rain pelting the roof like marbles from the sky. I got out of bed, grabbed an ice-cold bottle of Coke and ran out to the front porch to enjoy the rain. We have not yet had a summer, or even a spring rain. The ground and air have been as dry and dusty as the inside of a vacuum bag.

Suddenly, as I sat on the front porch in the old rocking chair, watching the rain pour out of the two valleys made by the house roof joining the porch roof, I was reminded of my best memory of hurricane Katrina. I remember that we came home to our house the day after the hurricane. The house and yard were a complete mess. It looked like everything in the yard had been picked up, put into a jar and vigorously shaken; then poured back out into the yard again, with extras from other people's yards. The same effect greeted us when we opened the front door of our house. The floors were covered in two inches of stinky sludge. Carpets were soaked and hardwood floors had blossomed into flowers of splinters and boards. Our furniture was completely re-arranged. The sofa was now in the center of the living room, instead of against the back wall. The cedar chest we had in the living room had floated into the bathroom. Not a single thing was dry or where we had left it and all was ruined.

I knew immediately that it was unsafe for my wife, daughter and mom to stay in the house. Regardless, the mess had to be cleaned immediately if we were to save the house. We began the process of removing debris from the inside of the home. I picked up chairs and sofas and dollied appliances into the front and back yards. I dumped them anywhere there was room.

The temperatures soared to triple digits. We had no electricity to run the AC that we're so accustomed to. The house became a sauna and the endless work of mucking out the house and trying to clean the floors became hell in itself. That evening, we lay exhausted on our soaked mattresses, begging for the temperature to drop so sleep would come. The following day early in the morning, my wife's cousin came to rescue my wife, daughter and mom from the terrible conditions in our home. He and a friend had driven from Jacksonville to take them out. It was difficult for me to say goodbye, because my daughter's third birthday was in three days and I would not be with her. Who knew how long it would be before I would see them again.

With the girls gone, the arduous task of mucking the house resumed, only now it was with full force and at maximum overdrive. I had to get the house cleared to save it from black mold and to get my family back home. For days I worked ripping out sheetrock and insulation, scrubbing floors, throwing out everything below the four-foot high-water line. I worked endlessly until I would sometimes collapse in the yard and rest in the shade, praying for relief from the intense heat.

After dark, the neighbors all gathered on Miss Agnes's' big ole cool front porch and talk about how our houses were coming along. It was so hot and dry as we sat fanning with cardboard and looking at the stars in the darkness. We wished and prayed for the rain to come and cool us off. We had no running water, and I know I must smell pretty strong, but couldn't really tell who's stink was the most distinguished, Albert's, Thomas, Danny, Fats or Dad's.

Nearly three weeks went by, dry as dust. One afternoon the rain came. Like this morning, the raindrops were big and vigorously pelted the house. I ran across the street where everyone was sitting on Miss Agnes's' porch to share the experience of rain at last. Though the debris pile in front of our yard was stacked twelve feet high, I could see the water running down the valley of our roof just like it's doing this morning.

I realized that after all these weeks of working in the muck and debris and heat that I had not showered or bathed in about two weeks. We were still without our utilities, including water, but not that day! A light bulb went off in my head that afternoon and I ran to our house and grabbed the soap and shampoo. I stripped to my boxers and jumped into the fabulous waterfall that runs from the roof besides the porch. As I scrubbed and glorified the waterfall that cleansed by body and refreshed my soul, I could see my neighbors watching. I bet they wished they had valleys like mine.

DQ, Bay St. Louis, MS

Hi! I'm DQ. I'm an eleven-year-old black kid who evacuated from the Mississippi Gulf Coast for Hurricane Katrina.

My Grandma and Grandpa took me and my Uncle Chris, who is a senior in high school, and we went to Meridian, Mississippi to get away from the storm. We stayed at a Motel 6 right off the Interstate. Grandma used to teach school and wants us to get our education, no matter what storm hits. The schools down home were a mess, so she put us in school here and we live in the motel.

Chris is not happy, because he wanted to graduate with the kids he always went to school with. I don't care, just so I get to play ball, too.

We have two rooms, My Grandma and Grandpa stay in one and Chris and me are in the other one. We have a cooler with water and sodas and stuff. Every day I have to empty out the water and go get ice at the machine by the stairs. There is one Queen-size bed in the room, a long dresser where we keep our clothes and a big mirror. Of course, there is a TV set. Chris brought his games and we play sometimes.

Chris has one of those big earrings. You know, the big kinda' diamond-looking one that you can't buy in stores. You gotta' get it from another black guy. It was for pierced ears. He left it on the dresser every day when he went to school but put it on when he goes to hang out after classes.

Well, one morning when he left for school, I had everything done already and was just sitting here looking around at the room. I saw his earring flashing over on the dresser. I opened up the cooler and got two pieces of ice. I put one on each side of my left ear lobe until it was all numb. I picked up the earring and pushed until I heard the 'pop' as it went through. I put the little holder on the end and then I heard my school bus crunch in the parking lot. I ran out fast before he could blow the horn and wake up my Grandma.

All the kids at the new school thought I was a Hip Hopper because I came to school wearing the big earring. I didn't mind. I was the new kid in school so I kinda' like everyone thinking I'm special. Wearing that big ole' diamond sure made me *feel* special.

I made sure to take the earring out and put it in my pocket before I got off the bus. I snuck it back on the dresser as soon as I got in the room. Chris was usually doing his homework and didn't notice. He probably never knew it was even missing. *Whew!*

That went on for a pretty good while. I'd just kind of not look at it when Chris was in the room. He never did know I wore it almost every day for weeks. One day I was talking with these kids on the school bus so much I forgot to take it out. So when I got off the bus and walked into the room, I saw Chris looking at me like he did and I knew I was in trouble.

"Take that off right now!" he said. "Don't ever let me catch you wearing my stuff again, either."

"Okay," I said, and I took the earring out and laid it in his hand. I don't think anyone else noticed me wearing it. I mean, my Grandma would'a fussed even more than Chris if she'd a seen it.

Observation

It has been a year since hurricane Katrina came ashore on the Mississippi Gulf Coast and devastated the entire southern region. The wave, which came ashore at a speed of 156mph, was compared to a tsunami with winds, torrential rains and tornadoes thrown in for good measure.

The shore still shows the ravages of the tidal wave, while the forested areas still have beaucoup deadwood that is a constant fire hazard, as well as a termite magnet. The people who live here smile and are glad things are progressing along. The volunteers who come from far away to help us gasp at the long way we still have to go.

Our pastor, Richard Jones says, "We got sat on by a great big elephant, named Katrina. You have come to take a bite out of that elephant."

The many, many bites taken out of the mess this past year are a blessing to all who call this place home. The trees have begun to branch out a bit, now that summer's almost over. They still look like they have poodle cuts, though. The lawns are coming along, slowly to be sure, because the man of the house has to hammer and nail instead of ride his mower on the weekends.

I would say the biggest obstacle has been finance. The grants and SBA loans are great, but this is a retirement community, and folks don't like to borrow what they may not be able to pay back. The groups who come down with wood, sheetrock, paint and stuff help most of all. My neighbor wouldn't be in her house today if it hadn't been for church organizations and other such groups hadn't pitched in for her. Imagine the cold fact of being homeless at age 86? It's all good. Without groups blessing us with loving kindness, backed up by solid wood and floor tile and windows, siding, etc. We'd be in pretty bad shape. Gone with the wind, so to speak.

The progress is visible, the heartbreak will heal and we have people like you to thank for it all. Without help from our friends in neighboring states, we would have starved to death, died of thirst, heat stroke and still be sleeping in our tents. There are no words enough to say "thank you".

The four months that Pawpaw and I spent at my daughter's house in Dillon, gave us the time to gather our strength and heal from our heartbreak while in the loving, supportive heart of family. It was such a blessing to be with someone who cares and goes to the trouble to make sure you are comfortable and have what you need. While there, I had cataract surgery on both eyes, and the doctors, nurses and receptionist were so kind. Joyce Samuels, manager of a little shop called Twice as Nice, made sure I found the clothing I needed to supplement my meager wardrobe. She gave me wonderful sales prices, knowing how little I had in the way of cash. What a blessing.

Getting to know my four grandsons, whom I'd only seen on occasional visits for the past ten years, was really a shock. What happened to those little babies? They grew up, of course. I was delighted when we watched James and Mitchell graduate from Dillon High School. And of course, I got to watch Joey graduate from elementary school and Joshua play football. It was all good.

Graduation

The end

www.ingramcontent.com/pod-product-compliance
Lightning Source LLC
Chambersburg PA
CBHW031251280526
45784CB00004B/1803